The Evolution
of Consciousness

The Evolution of Consciousness

Navigating the Levels of Awareness and Unlocking Spiritual Potential

David R. Hawkins, M.D., Ph.D.

HAY HOUSE LLC
Carlsbad, California • New York City
London • Sydney • New Delhi

Published in the United States by: Hay House LLC: www.hayhouse.com®
Published in Australia by: Hay House Australia Publishing Pty Ltd: www.hayhouse.com.au
Published in the United Kingdom by: Hay House UK Ltd: www.hayhouse.co.uk
Published in India by: Hay House Publishers (India) Pvt Ltd: www.hayhouse.co.in

Cover design: Julie Davison
Interior design: Stefan Killen, Red+Company

Cataloging-in-Publication Data is on file at the Library of Congress

Tradepaper ISBN: 978-1-4019-7708-5
E-book ISBN: 978-1-4019-7709-2

10 9 8 7 6 5 4 3 2 1
1st edition, October 2024

Printed in the United States of America

This product uses responsibly sourced papers and/or recycled materials. For more information, see www.hayhouse.com.

The original titles of the audio lecture series are *The Levels of Consciousness: Subjective & Social Consequences* and *Positionality and Duality: Transcending the Opposites.*

Map of Consciousness®

God-view	Life-view	Level		Log	Emotion	Process
Self	Is	Enlightenment	⇑	700-1000	Ineffable	Pure Consciousness
All-Being	Perfect	Peace	⇑	600	Bliss	Illumination
One	Complete	Joy	⇑	540	Serenity	Transfiguration
Loving	Benign	Love	⇑	500	Reverence	Revelation
Wise	Meaningful	Reason	⇑	400	Understanding	Abstraction
Merciful	Harmonious	Acceptance	⇑	350	Forgiveness	Transcendence
Inspiring	Hopeful	Willingness	⇑	310	Optimism	Intention
Enabling	Satisfactory	Neutrality	⇑	250	Trust	Release
Permitting	Feasible	Courage	⇕	200	Affirmation	Empowerment
Indifferent	Demanding	Pride	⇓	175	Scorn	Inflation
Vengeful	Antagonistic	Anger	⇓	150	Hate	Aggression
Denying	Disappointing	Desire	⇓	125	Craving	Enslavement
Punitive	Frightening	Fear	⇓	100	Anxiety	Withdrawal
Disdainful	Tragic	Grief	⇓	75	Regret	Despondency
Condemning	Hopeless	Apathy	⇓	50	Despair	Abdication
Vindictive	Evil	Guilt	⇓	30	Blame	Destruction
Despising	Miserable	Shame	⇓	20	Humiliation	Elimination

CONTENTS

INTRODUCTION

When Dr. David R. Hawkins presented the March and April 2002 lectures offered in this book, he was excited to share this information that would remove the obstacles and misperceptions, clearing the upward path for anyone interested in spiritual growth and enlightenment. The work was new, groundbreaking, and growing in recognition. The discovery that there now was a way to tell truth from falsehood was both miraculous and extremely beneficial. He says:

> The realization that you can tell truth from falsehood is so profound that hardly anybody gets the implication. At no time in human history has there been any way to tell truth from falsehood, whatsoever. . . . . To be able to tell the difference between truth and falsehood is enormous, profound. Its implications, its applications, and just about everything in society, is profound. (March 2002 lecture)

Because of his love for humankind, Dr. Hawkins's purpose was to impart this material and share his spiritual experiences in a way that was clear, credible, attainable, and helpful.

In your hands is the second book of a six-book series, from the 2002 lecture series, *The Way to God*. As you read you will understand in more detail:

PART 1:

- Muscle Testing: a way to tell truth from falsehood

- What do they mean: the linear and nonlinear domains

1

- The levels of consciousness: a detailed description
- Forgiveness: an important aspect of spiritual work
- What is the difference between Enlightenment and Salvation?
- The Meaning of Context and Content

PART 2:

- How to recontextualize the Ego: it is not necessary to hate or destroy it
- Transcend the opposites by transcending positionalities
- Moving in Consciousness is a "shift in quality"
- Consciousness is really the appearance of love and the evolution of love
- Enlightenment and progressive Divine levels of Consciousness
- The absolute benevolence of Divinity is that by one's own choice one determines one's own karmic destiny

These are just some of the many topics that Dr. Hawkins talks about using visual aids, examples, and his lightheartedness and sense of humor.

As he says: "One of the most healing modalities useful in spiritual work is a sense of humor."

We hope you will grow in leaps and bounds as you read this inspiring book.

Susan Hawkins and the Veritas Staff

Part I

THE LEVELS OF CONSCIOUSNESS: SUBJECTIVE & SOCIAL CONSEQUENCES

CHAPTER 1

THE MAP OF CONSCIOUSNESS® AND SOCIETY

We decided to give a series of 12 lectures, so I will then have said everything I have to say, and I can rest peacefully in the great beyond, you see. I don't want at the last moment to say, *Oh, gosh, I forgot to tell them all about it.* That's a good rule of thumb, you know, for spiritual decisions—is, what do you want to be responsible for on your deathbed? I remember making a number of decisions in my life because the last moment is really quite a confrontation.

Every lecture is really complete in a way, but the emphasis is different, and we'll have questions and answers throughout.

The Map of Consciousness®

Here we're emphasizing the Map of Consciousness® as it applies: what it is; what is the world; and then how that relates in general to the whole field of consciousness. You're aware that consciousness, in the writings that I've been doing, can roughly be defined as the *linear* and the *nonlinear*—the linear being the ego, the world of form, definition, that which is temporal, that which the world believes as reality; as compared—and this is just a point of perception—it's not a different level, but compared to the nonlinear, which is not definable as form, is considered by a large percentage of the world to be unreal; and it's classically defined as spiritual.

The Map of Consciousness® crosses over between the two. The importance of the book *Power vs. Force* was—after 30 years of not saying anything about this subject at all, I suddenly became an expert—how to define, how to make it possible to go from the known to the unknown. The radical subjectivity of a spiritual state is difficult to describe, and as I say, for 30 years I never mentioned it. And then saw this medical test called "kinesiology." It was considered a medical test. When I saw John Diamond do that kinesiology, instantly I saw what it was, because my reality already was nonlinear, and therefore I saw it from a different dimension from the rest of the audience. It was always presumed to be a local phenomena where a local condition causes a local reaction; and I saw that it was a nonlinear phenomena, and that the reaction was due to the presence of a nonlinear state of consciousness. So, it opened then, that kinesiology could be used beyond the linear and beyond the local, and in experimenting with it over many years now, we found that we had a means of directly accessing a field called "consciousness," which is, again, very iffy to people who live in the Newtonian paradigm of reality. The "consciousness" in that definition is whether you're awake or asleep.

Consciousness, in the spiritual definition, of course, is the field, the field from which one is aware of one's existence. And the context of mind is the field, and it's not the content. So, the world, the ordinary world, lives in the world of content, takes the subjective for granted without appreciating what it actually is. The subjective is where we exist. Our knowingness, our awareness that we "are" or that anything else "is," is only because of a radical state of subjectivity. It's roughly called "awareness," "consciousness," and the thing that differentiates it from the Newtonian paradigm is that the subjective has no content. So, we might say that the world is . . . Let's say, if computers had arms and legs and were walking around, the computers in the ordinary world would all think that they are their software. They'd say, "I'm Mr. QuickBooks. Glad to meet you. And you're Miss IRS Computer Form number 660, glad to meet you." And then there would be a maverick in the midst of all of them who walks around and says, "Well, I'm my hardware;

I'm none of those things." And they would consider him slightly insane and put him off in a corner. So, if he's wise, he doesn't mention that—and I never did for 30 years: that I'm my hardware and the software comes and goes. The one reality behind all computers is, without hardware, there are no software programs possible. The world thinks it's its programs.

We're going to talk about those programs and, of course, illuminate the whole understanding of consciousness itself, as a consequence. Most everybody here has read *Power vs. Force*, or maybe *The Eye of the I*. Either way, the Map of Consciousness® has become extremely well-known; it's widely quoted, and I get requests every day to reprint it in some publication or article. It's become a useful tool. So, we should understand what it really reflects. What does it really reflect? As we will see, it's a way of describing the ego, is really what it is. If we look at society . . . we were talking about the Map of Consciousness® as it is expressed in today's society.

If we look at the world and society, what we see is the ego projected out there. The world itself is a playground, a graveyard, an amusement center, depending on your point of perception. So, I consider it entertainment. It's sort of like turning on the TV. Yesterday morning's newspaper was dramatic—it had two of the most horrible stories you could possibly read, and it just broke me up because it's like the world pushes the extreme just like TV programs do, push the extreme.

When I was a kid, my grandmother would always read the newspaper, and then she would cry. She would always find a sad story and cry. And my grandfather would get very irritated with her. "Molly, will you cut that out!" Life is a theater of the absurd.

So, we'll talk about these levels of consciousness to get them clarified once and for all, what they mean, and clear up any confusions that there could be about it. To begin with, they are neither better nor worse. It is not a hierarchy of worthiness or accomplishment. It is a way of looking like a prism. A prism breaks up the light into its different colors. It doesn't mean that ultraviolet is better than blue or better than green. What we've done here is break up the levels of consciousness with a prism, and these would be the colors that come out. So, these colors, what they are is progressive levels of power within the field of consciousness, first of all. The higher you go, the greater the power. To some degree, it's like a thermometer. And on this thermometer, these are various degrees of power, and there are also various degrees of love. They also are various degrees to which, you might say, the presence of God is consciously reflected into life.

To transcend the opposites, it's necessary to give up a positionality. And we use a thermometer as an example. You can't just put your finger here and say, "Above it is 'hot,' and below it's 'cold'; and now 'hot' and 'cold' are opposites." That's what the mind does. We will take this up in a lecture on "Transcending the Opposites." To reach the so-called state of enlightenment, it's necessary to drop all positionalities in which duality disappears. And that is the pathway of Advaita, which we'll have a lecture on, and in dropping of positionality. So, the presence of God as it is manifested— as in the Manifest—and radiates through a specific consciousness, then, we would say at the top that the light is clearer, that there's less darkness in the field, and that's why they are called "enlightened" states. Their light actually is almost an experiential one; it's almost like a great clarity, and light does diffuse everything.

As the ego imposes itself between truth and its own egocentricity—we might say that the bottom is egocentricity. So, if the top is God, what is the bottom? The bottom is profound states of egocentricity, out of which considerable damage to the world— the world can count, in our view of it. Let's say, Mr. Bin Laden calibrates at 70, which is down in here, and so, that which is below tends to bring what we consider somewhat destructive, but that, of course, is a point of view. It was constructive from his viewpoint. So, again, "constructive" and "destructive" are positionalities.

The levels of consciousness, however, we were able to calibrate using kinesiology. I forget how we even started with it, but the levels are really traditional; that's really a perennial philosophy, only documented, and I being brought up as a psychiatrist and a psychoanalyst and psychoanalyzed, I naturally applied these things as I understood life and the human mind. These are states that are both emotional and intellectual and spiritual; and these are the names by which we commonly know these phenomena in daily life: anger, fear, grief, pride, hope—all those things. Then, to give it an additional usefulness, it's been calibrated, and the calibrations turned out to be logarithms. So, a move of a few points on the scale, as you're aware, in a log is 10 to that number—so it's a very sizable move. The move from, let's say, from 200 to 202 does not sound like much numerically, but because you're talking about the logarithm, it is 10 to the 202nd power rather than the 200th power. Numerically, that's quite a difference.

Where is that in society? Well, we found that most government agencies calibrate about 202. Yes, 200 is the level of integrity. So, we said 200 and over—we made the interesting discovery that 200 and over that some things made you go strong and then some things made you go weak. So we discovered kinesiologically, then, consciousness is aware of the difference between truth and falsehood; between that which is pro-life and that which is detrimental to life. And on a scale of 1 to 1000, we would say, on 1 to 1000, what is this dividing line? It came out 200. We'd say, "Is it over 150?" So, these numbers were arrived at pragmatically by discovery; their value is relative. Their value is relative. Anybody can make up their own scale. You can make up a scale 1 to 10; you can make up a scale 1 to 100; you can make up your own scale.

If you're going to do calibrations and try to arrive at numbers to compare to this Map, you have to sort of preface it with: "As compared to this Map, so-and-so (or something) calibrates over 200." Some people don't do that, and they come up with strange numbers—that their baby calibrates over 2000, and things. They send me excited telegrams. They do, literally. We get faxes and phone calls, stuff around the clock. A newborn baby, 1200 or something. Whoa, the Baby Jesus just re-emerged. So, if you're not getting the same number—it's a relative scale; it's not an absolute scale. It's useful; it is profoundly useful. On the one hand, you can ignore it completely and just trust and love God, and that's sufficient. That's so. You don't have to do any of this. But being a human being with a mind, it's probably not going to satisfy you to do that. And as somebody said to me, "It's also quite boring." This does add some entertainment on the way. It's better than saying the rosary thousands of times, which can be very boring if you've ever tried it, and you get up to a thousand, and it's like a drop-over deal.

The world, then, is interesting. In the books that I'm writing, I sometimes cite events in the world, and people say, "Why are you saying something about the world?" It's not because I am concerned about the world. It's because it reflects the ego. When you read the daily newspaper, you're seeing your own ego projected out there. It's really a neat teaching tool. I love the evening news, because it's hysterically entertaining and because you see the games the ego's playing: the ego speaks through this person's mouth and then this person's mouth, you know what I mean? "It is a violation of our civil rights to . . ." Or say, "In God we trust." We could say, "In God we don't trust." Or we could say, "We don't trust in anybody." How's that? Forget trust. I mean you can't bring up a thing without a political angle . . . you know what I'm saying?

We found that there was a critical level. This is known in foreign cultures. When we were in Korea, they said that's the way they buy a tangerine in the store. If the tangerine makes you go strong, you buy it; if it makes you go weak—they don't buy it. Commonly known. Based on the strict, obvious physiologic basis that "all that is" has certain characteristics. Protoplasm withdraws from that which is noxious. It bleeds if you stick a needle in it. That's impersonal. These calibrated fields are impersonal. The kinesiologic test is impersonal.

Right now, Susan and I, we're working on a book which is going to have a thousand calibrations: anything and everything that is on the planet that ever meant anything. From Cicero, Nero, to the Pietà, to Westminster Abbey, to all the great beings, throughout the *Great Books of the Western World*, et cetera.

So these calibrations are very pragmatic; they are very useful. They are radically useful. Because it tells the difference between truth and falsehood. It was devastating. And a few people who first reviewed the book were totally devastated. One man took off, went to Europe and spent two weeks to recover from the shock. The realization that you can tell truth from falsehood is so profound that hardly anybody gets the implication. At no time in human history has there been any way to tell truth from falsehood whatsoever. We see all kinds of approximations, the scientific method and all these desperate attempts, to tell what Susan and I can tell in a second. You look at the IRS form—and I said, "Well, I think it takes an average of sixteen hours to fill it out, or something like that." Or we can say, "We owe them over 2000, 3000, 4000, 4400—there we go." We send them a check. "We checked with kinesiology, and this is what we owe you."

Truth vs. Falsehood

To be able to tell the difference between truth and falsehood is enormous, profound. Its implications, its applications, and just about everything in society is profound. In the daily news, there's always a war someplace, and in every war, the United States, for some reason, never knows what's happening. The U.S. is always surprised—surprised by Pearl Harbor, by attacks in Afghanistan. They are always surprised and never seem to know what's happening. So, its implication is to not know is to be vulnerable, and to know is a much better position to be in. It would be better to know how many soldiers are hiding in the caves there than to walk in with a half dozen people and find you're surrounded by a thousand, or something.

The usefulness is very, very pragmatic in daily life. Lots of times a question will come up and we just ask kinesiology, and we get yes or no, and that solves it. You notice that a lot of people are very familiar with this thing, and we have talked about it before, so I don't want to spend undue time on it. However, the critical point is whether a thing is over 200 or below 200. You don't need to know the number. Either a thing makes you go strong with kinesiology, or it makes you go weak.

Now, how accurate is the test itself? I'm not a kinesiologist. There are many people who are experts; they do it all day, every day, and they're very, very adept at it. They know various techniques. There's the O-ring technique, where you can pull and see and compare how strong you're holding Jesus in mind and how strong you are holding a person in mind, and get a yes or no. We say, generally, if it's an important question, we like kinesiology with two people. One reason is, if you can find somebody you can work with—and that can be a problem—a lot of married couples cannot work with each other; they have to find some other person, for reasons I'm not sure. But if you can find somebody you can work with and you work with them consistently—if you're involved with it in a sort of very serious way, what happens is, the person you work with becomes strangely attuned to your question. Almost as I walk over to ask, a knowingness comes on, and the answer is there; in fact, I can feel it run down my arm as I ask it. You become quite adept at it after a while. The person that works with you gets to almost intuitively tune in to—I'm searching for something and I have no clue to it, and suddenly she'll say, "What about the so-and-so?" And we ask, and, yes, that's what we're looking for. The value of having a partner is that their intuition is added to yours, and you can accomplish a rather formidable task in very short order.

There are people who are trained in it. There are techniques that are well demonstrated in videos, books, and audiotapes. *Switched-On Living* is done by Jerry Teplitz.

So, as I say, I'm not a kinesiologist. My only interest—like, Galileo's interest in telescopes was that you could see out there, but he wasn't really a telescope maker; it wasn't really his thing. We refer questions on the techniques out to people who are good at it. In many communities, chiropractors are the best at it. They use it more extensively than holistic doctors. It's an extremely useful technique—"yes" or "no." People say, "Well, can I get the same answers with dowsing?" The answer is, generally, yes. Generally, yes—as far as a yes-or-no answer.

The calibrated levels, then, have enormous significance. In doing the most important events, people, and places in all of human history, you get almost a topographical map. You begin to get an understanding of human history that you're not capable of getting from just dry, linear facts, or even from travelogues. You begin to see how consciousness evolves. In the book I'm just finishing, *I*, I try to track the evolution of consciousness throughout time and throughout all of evolution up to its present point in the emergence of a new level of consciousness, a new kind of humanity.

Out of *Homo sapiens*, we see what *Homo sapiens* have been up to the last several thousand years. Before that we had Cro-Magnon man, and we had Neanderthal man—and you see I'm not politically correct; I don't call them "Neander." I call them "Neander-*thal*." I grew up with Neanderthal, and that's going to have to be good enough! Anyway, the most important thing we discovered for mankind in general was that the level of mankind went from 190, where it had been for many, many centuries, and went to 207 about 1986. That began, then, the emergence of a whole new paradigm of what's possible for mankind despite today's headline news. And it signaled to me, anyway, the emergence of a new paradigm of reality, and it signaled the emergence of a new branch off the evolutionary tree, which I call *Homo spiritus*. *Homo sapiens* did not have spiritual awareness. *Homo sapiens* have been busy killing each other and murdering each other and drowning each other for centuries and centuries and centuries. Killing each other off at the rate of 70 million lives in one big sweep in World War II.

Now, a new emergence is the dominance, then, of a positive spiritual energy dominating the consciousness field of mankind. So, what you could get away with, what was acceptable in past times—in past times, it was assumed if you captured an enemy, naturally you enslaved them, raped them, pillaged them, and killed them, and often mutilated them in horrible ways. And that was considered okay: "It's the way the world is," and nobody questioned it. At a consciousness level of 207, there would be a cry of outrage, an outrage—the fact that our consciousness has now emerged. So, a new emergence of awareness is dominating the whole field of human consciousness, with profound implications for everyone.

So, 200, then, denotes the difference—and again, it is not a level of opposites. It's not that 200 and above is one reality and below 200 is another reality. It's not good versus bad. Remember, this is a thermometer, and the presence of God, the presence of Love, is what accounts for the calibration. Above this level, you go strong, and below goes weak. It looks like you're looking at true and false; it looks like you're looking at good and evil. But that is not the case. The case is that . . . you see, water—water is still water whether it is ice, liquid, or steam. The only thing that changes there is temperature. Above this temperature, you got over 212 degrees Fahrenheit; it changes its quality. Then, below 212 degrees Fahrenheit, it turns back into liquid, changes its quality, but it's still just water. Then, at 32 degrees Fahrenheit, it changes its quality and turns into a solid. So you can't say steam is the *opposite* of ice or that water is the *opposite* of steam. As the temperature increases or decreases, then quality changes.

There's not two different things—light and dark. There is intense light; as the light gets lower and lower and lower, it gets dimmer and dimmer and dimmer; then it gets harder and harder to see, and we say it's dusk or dark. There's only one variable, and that's light, the presence of light. That's the only variable. There's not two things, light and dark. You can't take a box of darkness and put it someplace and say, "Shine me some darkness in this closet." It doesn't have any existence. The only reality, then, is light, and light is either present or not present, and it's present in varying degrees. So, the analogy is that the Love of God is like the light. Up on the Map of Consciousness˚, the Love of God is quite intense, and down below, it diminishes and becomes progressively darker.

When this happens, the human emotion that goes with it, goes through the whole panorama. From an ecstatic state, there's a state beyond ecstasy, a blissful state of absolute serenity and stillness. As the calibrated levels come down, you see the shift of emotions. Below 200, we notice that these emotions are classically negative and painful. And down at the bottom, they become quite severe. They even lead to suicide.

The interesting thing about calibrated levels of conscious- · ness is that everybody has a calibrated level of consciousness the instant they're born. The instant they're born, there's already a calibratable level of consciousness, which has a certain implication. We'll have another lecture in which we talk just about karma itself. Either life is extremely unfair or there's a coherence, and a spiritual coherence to the universe, in which case there is no such thing as "accidental." In a coherent universe in which the presence of God is the infinite context out of which all reality arises, there is no such thing as an accident. *Accident*, like the word *chaos*, means a limitation of perception. It means from the Newtonian point of view, it looks like an accident. But from the overall point of view, there are no accidents possible.

The Infinite Reality of God

The infinite reality of God, then, is like an infinite electromagnetic field. Its power is absolute. Its power is unlimited. Its power is infinite. All That Is, is held within the infinite power of the infinite context of God. Nothing can happen outside of it. Consequently, an accident is not possible. For an accident to be so, it would have to be outside the infinite context of the universe, and if it was there, you wouldn't know it. So, no accident is possible. Everything falls within a coherence. Each thing is where it is because of what it is. Each thing becomes the fulfillment of its own essence, and in so doing, its characteristics define where it will position itself within the overall infinite field of power. So, you see, nothing is causing anything. Everything is just being what it is. As a consequence of its being what it is, it automatically moves in an infinite field of power.

It's important to understand that, because we want to get it past the barriers of picturing God as some kind of a judgmental, arbitrary being. People fear death, because now you're going to meet the great judgmentalism. So, each thing is where it is, and it's being what it is because out of creation, its essence then defines that if it has wings, it flies, you see? But that's coming out its own essence. Those who seek God do so out of the evolution of their own consciousness, because the quality of consciousness is to progressively seek to know its own nature.

Karmic Unity

I've been asked, if there are no accidents, then, does that make us predestined, in a sense? That question always arises. The entire universe is one karmic unity. People say, "Do you believe in karma?" It's not a matter of believing in karma. The entire universe is one infinite coherence, the context of which has infinite power, because the power arises out of context. Therefore, out of the infinite potentiality that we tend to call God arises the entire universe as an obvious coherence. So each thing, then—what occurs is a result of the essence of its own reality. Each thing, then, you might say, has its own karma within the infinite coherence of the universe. Nothing can fall outside the universe, so consequently, everything within the universe is subject to the laws of the universe. Each thing, then, is a result of what it is. Spiritually, what it is, is the accumulated result of its own decisions by its own spiritual will. By one's own spiritual will, one rises or falls like a cork in the water. Each moment we choose instant by instant. To constantly choose in one direction, to constantly choose the direction of the light, eventuates constantly going higher on the Map of Consciousness°. To refuse the light, which is your privilege—and everyone is created free; one can refuse God, refuse the Love of God; one can condemn God; one can curse God and thereby choose the dark. The dark is by one's own choice. And those who ridicule God will then go to realms occupied by those who ridicule God. If we calibrate them, they're not where you want to go. And that's what Jesus said: you don't want to go there. He said it's not wrong; it's just that you don't really want to go where the sinful go when they die. And the Buddha said the same. And every great religion and spiritual teacher tells you the same thing; that you really do not want to go there.

Anybody who has ever been in profound guilt, shame, agony, depression, and loss; or terror; or hopeless rage—those are the approaches to hell, and then you get to where it really gets bad. So the great teachers have advised us that it's not where you want to go, and that is a correct statement. So, it's not that we're pre-destined, because predestination sounds arbitrary. You can only be that which you are. Let me answer it that way. By the nature of existence and beingness, one can only be what one is. What one is, one has sculpted by one's own hand. Therein lies the infinite justice of God.

These emotions, then, as they go up the scale become increas-ingly agreeable. These are low on the Map; everybody comes to see the doctor in these states. This is my office down here: despair, anxiety, depression, angriness. People don't see me out of arro-gance, but—yeah, they do. Anyway, as we go up, we see the levels are far more . . . and that's because the process is different. Here, at the level of integrity, you have the true beginning of empower-ment at 200. Below that, you get inflation. The reason I don't like political correctness is because it calibrates at 190 and has a grat-ing "holier than thou" superiority about it, and its results don't verify it. So there's an ego inflation, egotism here. Over here at the lower levels, the ego, like, shrinks, you see. But here at 190, it's inflamed and pridefulness. Here we have the anger; anger gives people a temporary sense of power. It's a false sense of power. It's the most difficult problem I have. I'm chief of staff at a big resi-dential place where we have 50 teenage girls. Their main problem is angriness, other than impulsivity, poor judgment, and getting into all kinds of horrible trouble. But on a day-to-day level, their getting along with each other is constantly impaired with angri-ness. They are always angry. They are like Johnny One-Note. No matter what happens, their only response is anger. If it's too cool in the room, they're angry about that; if it's too warm, they're angry about that. If I mention a certain subject, they're angry about that, and if I don't, they're angry because I didn't mention it. It's just a proneness to angriness.

Power and Force

If you don't have any power, these are all levels of weakness. If you don't have any real power, then the next thing to do is inflate yourself. So you see the puffed-up arrogance of Slobodan Milosevic, former president of Serbia. When they take his picture, he's always got his head up: "The U.N. and all the countries of the world have no right to question what I do." From 200 down are really levels of weakness, and 200 over are levels of power. If you have real power, you don't need all that. It's like self-esteem. If you lack self-esteem, you feel you need self-esteem. If you have self-esteem, you don't need self-esteem, and you're not even interested in it, you know. If people think you're fine, you're glad they're happy; and if they don't think you're fine, then it's their problem. What people think about you is sort of irrelevant, because you're autonomous. So, these people under 200 are not autonomous. What people think about them makes a very big difference. Because these are levels of weakness, then; these are levels of force.

Up above 200, you have power. Power just stands there by itself. Power influences everything within its domain as a consequence of that which it is. That which you are has a more profound effect on everything than that which you do. That's sort of the meaning of the spiritual teacher who says, "Don't worry about saving the world. Save yourself." Because with the evolution of your own consciousness—you are already doing more for mankind than you can do out there with placards and "Take God out of business," or whatever it is, whatever it is. The world you see is just a story, a perceptual story as witnessed by the ego, and therefore there's nothing out there that needs saving. Don't waste your time saving the world. Save yourself, because thereby you radiate forth that which has a profound influence.

You see, force always results in counterforce. Force goes from here to there and requires counterforce. It exhausts itself. Sooner or later, the troops on this side and the troops on *this* side are going to deplete their resources! In due time, they die by the millions. Therefore, force is relatively weak. And it's what the world relies on—the world relies on force. Those who have enormous power don't need to bother with force. So, these people under 200 resort to force because they lack power. Inflation makes you feel important. Being aggressive and angry makes you feel . . . the animal swells up with anger, and he puffs up there and he goes, "Boom, boom, boom!" and he tries to intimidate. Power, you get it in a flick of an eyebrow. I would do something and look at my father—a flick of his eyebrow, and instantly I'd behave differently. He didn't have to beat me, threaten me, anything. It's because of where we were, probably a mutuality on a certain level. The slightest flick of the eyebrow was sufficient, and still is for me. All a person has to do is say, "Unh," and I got it right away. I got it.

At the lower levels, the people become enslaved, they become addicted. This is the level of cravingness. This is wantingness. Up here you are arrogant; here you hate everybody, you're angry at everybody. 125 is the level of wantingness. This comes out of the solar plexus, just as the higher levels come out of the crown chakra and the third eye, and we get to love: the heart. Now we're down to the solar plexus. The solar plexus is also the level of courage. You have to have a lot of guts to get out there in the world. But if you get caught in it, too much energy in the solar plexus, you get into cravingness and wantingness. The difficulty with this is, you can never satisfy it. You buy this, it satisfies you for the moment—but tomorrow you'll want that, and the next day you'll want *that*. It's endless. It can lead, of course, to the addiction of drugs and alcohol, sexual addictions, the cravingness for power and wealth and worldly goods, and things like that. Or it can be a craving for experience and novelty—chasing sexual partners and racking up a score and various things; craving adulation of the public. So the cravingness is difficult because it's not satisfiable; there's no end point. That which is real has an end point. You strive for this, you get it, and now you're satisfied. But here, there's never satisfaction. You read about these people who have $200 million, and then they rip off their country for another $200 million. Then they rip off their business for $300 million and make all the stock owners probably say, "He's got three hundred million. Why does he need more?" I don't know what you do with $300 million! It would be an enormous nuisance, if you ask me—baggage! Why do they want more and more? Or you read about a robber like John Dillinger. He robbed a bank and got $28,000. Thursday, he's robbing another bank in another town. Even as a kid, I wondered, *Why does Dillinger need more money? He couldn't have spent it since last Thursday!* But the next Thursday, he's robbing another bank. Then a week later, it would be another town. I lived in the Midwest, and my mother was always afraid of John Dillinger; we would lock the doors at night because John Dillinger was loose. He was always robbing another bank and another store. What did he need all that money for? He's already got this old car, and he's got gas in it. I mean, what does he want with all this? There's no end to that.

Below that you start to handle fear itself. We said desire is cravingness. Under that is a fear, and fear runs most of the world, most of the time. Fear. The number of fears—to say to conquer a fear doesn't really solve it, because fearfulness is a state of consciousness, and it will just invent new things to be afraid of: afraid of tomorrow, afraid of yesterday catching up with them. So, fearfulness is a lack of faith in God, and one lives in constant fear. When they withdraw and become despondent, as we go down [on the Map] we see the eventuality of depression, despair, the giving-upness of hopelessness. Out of the pridefulness, then, underneath there's anger, the wantingness.

Now, the direction that you move is what's important. It's not where you're at. It isn't bad that you're low on the Map and good that you're higher. Maybe subjectively, experientially, it is. What's important is what direction you're moving. The great value of television is that the third-world countries that lived in apathy—when television came on in the poor neighborhoods all over the world, people that were in apathy saw all the beautiful things on TV. "Gee, how Americans live," and all that. "Wow!" Out of that came desire. Out of apathy, they began to *want*, to come out of hopeless apathy . . . What's hopeless apathy? You don't pick up the garbage on the streets. You don't give a damn about anything. You don't bother getting auto insurance. If you get a ticket, you don't bother going to court. Apathy is like uselessness. It's very hard to handle. Uselessness leads to more uselessness. And it becomes that whole subcultures are based in uselessness.

If you get that person, then, out of apathy and up to desire, now you can get him up to anger. Hey! Now they're angry. "All the have-nots have it, and I don't have it. And we'll bomb America and get even with them because they have it and we don't have it." Anyway, out of this anger, then, out of the anger, you get more energy. Then out of the beginning of pridefulness, you have the courage to face the reality of what it takes: what it takes to get out of apathy and poverty and not-havingness, to havingness.

Well, when people find out what it takes, they change their story a little bit. Because I counsel a lot of those people. They want to stay in the bed in the morning. I said, "No, you can't in this world. You have to get up at six o'clock in the morning, even if it's cold and dark out. You have to get dressed, and you have to travel to school or to work." "Oh, I ain't going to bother with that," they say. Well, you can't have it both ways, folks. Courage is facing biting the bullet that, yes, you *do* have to force yourself to get up. That's why we have alarm clocks. Of course you'd rather stay in bed and listen to the radio, et cetera. So, this is biting the bullet.

Real Power and Prior Karma

So, 200 is a very critical level. What you get in return is, now—instead of coming out of weakness and the utilization of force—you come into real power. Real power now begins to totally change your life. People react to you differently, respond to you different-ly. Your intentions tend to manifest within the world. A friend of mine who's moving upward rather rapidly spiritually said to me just the other day—he said, "Gee, I was holding exactly what I wanted from this guy in my mind. I wanted this, this, and this, and the other thing. I ran into the guy, and he instantly said to me, 'You know what I think I want to do for you? I want to do this, this, this, and this.' That's exactly what I was thinking—and I about fell over!" That's a subjective experience. So, what you hold in mind now tends to manifest, and therefore comes the saying: "Be careful of what you hold in mind, because it tends to materialize." As you move up and become more powerful, it does tend to materialize.

Down here near the bottom, we have starvation; at 20 or so, there's barely enough life energy to pull to you that which you need to survive. To be born into this world with a calibrated level of 25 means you will probably be born someplace where your parents will have certain diseases; you'll probably be dead, by the age of six months, of starvation. Level 20 has not got what it takes to pull nurturance to it. It totally lacks power. It's why you can't cure poverty with money, because poverty is a reflection of a level of consciousness. It will always pull poverty to it.

Because most people who attend these lectures are conditioned by a meritocracy, in which we assume moving upward and forward is what life is all about. There are people who are born, don't ask me why, at a consciousness level of 25. There's one place where I go and see patients. The consciousness level of the patient population there is 35; 35 is the consciousness level of the population there. So, some people are born to a low level of consciousness. The answer we get when testing is prior karma. You can argue with that; I don't care if you believe it.

Because of prior karma, they arrive at a level of 25 or 30. Maybe, then, in the lifetime as a warrior, when you slaughtered the captives instead of allowing them and giving them some kind of freedom, if it was your choice, you could let them live or not live, and you let them all die. The consequence could be that you blocked off the light further and further and further until now, you yourself are an entity that vibrates either with or without a physical body at 35. That entity, that entity vibrates at 35. Whether it's in or out of the body is relatively immaterial. If it's out of a body, it'll experience the hells in other domains. If it materializes in this world time, in this world, it's going to be low on the Map.

So, spiritual work, then, is making choices that move us up toward the light. So, that's all we do in spiritual work. The whole use of this scale, the whole use of what we learn from it, is merely to support the intention on the part of everyone here to move forward in consciousness and to fulfill the human potential. Being a human being is extremely difficult.

The Evolution of Life

And if you look at the whole evolution of life on this planet, you see it coming up from a germ plasm on up through primitive life forms. You see, the energy field of 70 is the energy field of the era of the dinosaur. The dinosaur is the rapacious energy that lives only by the destruction of others. The dinosaur only is alive because it kills you. It lives by the death of others. Later on in evolution, we see that the dinosaur finally killed itself off.

And we saw the emergence of the herbivore. We saw the emergence of a whole different line of evolution. The herbivore does not live by the killing of anybody or any other thing or any other entity. In fact, the herbivores that eat the grass take the oxygen, the sunshine, the chlorophyll that the plants have put together, and turn it into fertilizer and make more grass. Herbivores don't kill anybody. They eat the top off the grass, but the roots still survive. So, we see the emergence of that which is benign. That which is benign does not have to kill for survival.

As we get above the line, we see the collective human karma then began to manifest and the evolution of higher levels of life. Cro-Magnon man, Neanderthal man, *Homo erectus*, finally *Homo sapiens*. *Homo sapiens* was not aware of much of anything yet. *Homo sapiens* knew more than *Homo erectus* but still was not a walking genius, by any means. It took hundreds of thousands of years; a slow, painful evolution. Then came the emergence of spiritual awareness. First, spiritual awareness was intuitive and began to ascribe events to the stars and the weather and then to mysterious entities called "gods," et cetera. Human consciousness then evolved to the point of greater spiritual awareness, and in so doing, it went through primitive forms, anthropomorphic gods and primitive gods, et cetera.

It finally reached a state, however, in which God became the ultimate symbol of morality, ethics, right and wrong. It became the yardstick for behavior. And guilt emerged—guilt, profound guilt. So, being a human being is extremely difficult, because the evolutionary tree of a human is via the animal. We are all made of bone and blood and meat. People say, "Do you eat meat or don't eat meat?" I say, "You *are* meat. Every lion knows *that*." Ask a lion what you are; he'll tell you—you are meat, you are dinner, you are lunch, as far as he's concerned.

The human brain is structured, based on the emergence of the animal. So, we see awareness coming up through the animal kingdom and becoming more and more complex; that complexity being the neuronal structures of the human brain. And the beginning of spiritual awareness now puts man in the most difficult—if you ask me—position possible. You have, on the one hand, animal instincts which run you, whether you like it or not, by the very structure of the brain that you inherit, and now you have spiritual awareness. The human being is balanced between the animal and the spiritual. So you can't just chop up your enemies with glee anymore. That throws you into a terrible guilt complex—it's against the law, it's illegal, et cetera. Now, the human being lives in a world, however, of possibility. The animal does not live in a world of possibility. The lion sees a rabbit running—there's no possibility except to eat the rabbit. What else can he do? He's not going to read the rabbit a book, you know what I mean? The animal side is instinctual. The animal side is built in—we're wired, it's wired into the human brain.

So, genetically you come onto this planet without remembering to ask to even do that. Nobody asked me. Do you remember being asked, "Do you want to get born this time?" I don't know, without being consulted. Speaking of politically correct, do you really think we should allow that to continue? Where are my rights? I wasn't even consulted . . . ! The most important fact is, I exist. No one even asked me about that, much less about being a male or a female, or what color. Nothing was asked. So, there you are. All of a sudden, you're here, and you've got this human brain; it's based on the animal brain.

The ego is, from a global understanding, the evolution of the animal. The ego, from here down below 200, is nothing but the animal. This is all animal, right? Today's headlines or newsreel you can see on any Monkey Island in any zoo. The world is Monkey Island—gimme, gimme; kill, kill, kill; rape, rape, rape. That's what you see on Monkey Island: the alpha male, the alpha female; jealousy, competition, territoriality, possessiveness, greed. All that runs the human domain is not different than the animal world. So, one way of looking at the ego, then, is to have compassion for it as your little animal. It is a little animal, and he gets mad.

Somebody cuts you off in traffic: *Ooh, that son of a . . . !* You gotta win, fight. The human brain is wired that way. So, what's the point of feeling guilty about it? There's no point in feeling guilty about it. There is no point in grieving about it. It's just the animal. So, the ego, then, is nothing but the animal. It gets labeled "evil," "bad," and all that, but if you forget all the labels, it's really just the animal. If you give up judgmentalism, you can just accept it for what it is and say, "Of course it wants to do that."

Anything good happens in my life, I say, "Okay, let's hear it from the ego." Something good happens, the spiritual ego comes right up and says, "Aren't you marvelous; isn't that wonderful?" You know what I mean? You know it's going to come right up there. That's what it does. Otherwise, we wouldn't call it the spiritual ego. It is doing what it is supposed to do. It's nothing but the animal. Millions and millions of years, it learned how to survive. That's what the animal in you is trained and supposed to do. If it wasn't successful, you wouldn't be here today. It's because you owe your life to the success of your animal predecessors—your success as a human being, not your Success with a capital *S*, or your fate, depending on how you look at it.

So, here you are, a spiritually aware being, stuck with animal instincts; they're wired, and they're in your hardware. The thalamic nuclei, the nuclei at the base of the brain where the big emotional limbic system comes out—it's automatic, it triggers. I can show somebody a flash card, your limbic system is going to go right off. The electroencephalogram shows that flash. You haven't even had a chance to say hello about it, yes or no—built in. Not only is the animal brain built in with all these negative emotions here on the Map, but at the very back of the brain, you have the old dinosaur brain. The reptilian brain is still at the back of the brain, right. Anybody knows anything about anatomy knows the back of the brain, the rhinencephalon. Sounds like something you don't want to meet in the dark at night. It sounds scary. The old, primitive, reptilian brain is still at the back of your head. Every evolution of the animal chain as it evolved is represented in some nucleus in your hypothalamus or your "phigalatorus"—take that! This is in your phigalatorus right here, and when it wiggles—"I don't know, Doctor, every time I look at him, I just shake all over." It sets off the phigalatorus into a scared thing, huh? Because her head says, "Enemy." Uh-oh, enemy!—prey-predator response.

The Evolution of Consciousness

Now what happens is, consciousness begins to evolve. We see the beginning of intelligence. I love that wonderful gray parrot that's at University of South Arizona. What's that parrot's name? I forget. Anyway, this parrot talks and thinks and can pick out colors, choices, numbers. She will say to him, "Get green cube." He goes over and gets the green cube. "Put down green cube. Get four red round." Oh, four red round. The parrot knows how to think already. And of course, you all know Koko, the gorilla who has quite a big vocabulary of 800 words or something like that and knows sign language. So, we see the emergence of thinkingness capacity. So, what we're talking about now is the emergence of the forebrain, the forebrain. The capacity to think. Present even in birds and becomes more and more complex. That gives you more ways to suffer now than you had ever thought of before! With a forebrain, man, you can feel guilty about everything from instant to instant: *Why did I say that? Why did I do this? Why did I wear this? Oh, golly, why didn't I bring my hat?* So now, the capacity for suffering increases enormously. On the other hand, the capacity for satisfaction does also.

We come out of the animal world, then . . . what I am trying to do is recontextualize the ego. The ego is not a "bad," it's not an "awful." It'll take you to terrible places. If you let it run you, it'll take you to terrible places. But it gets scary labels put on it in the spiritual and religious worlds; it gets scary words: "sin" and "evil," and oh my god—now you lay awake at night worrying about all that stuff. The animal naturally wants to be right. The animal naturally wants to win. The animal doesn't care about other animals. It would just as soon kill it and take over its prey, take over its mate, take over its territory.

So, you know what Freud called the "id." What is in the id is the animal. Based on our profound spiritual premise of "let go resisting things," you let go resisting it. Instead of suppressing and repressing it or denying it, what mankind does is repress all this, deny it because of guilt, and project it into the world. He did not eliminate it; he just moved it "out there." Well, it's much nicer to feel that they're the bad guy and you're not the bad guy—they're the ones. There're all kinds of columnists who start blaming America by virtue of the fact that you save your money, work hard, and get out of bed in the morning instead of laying in the bed, and learned how to use the wheel and count—now we should get killed, see.

I've been in parts of the world where the wheel hasn't really been used. I was in the top of the Andes, and they were still dragging things around with sticks—so help me, God. That was in the '70s. Like they hadn't heard of the wheel yet. Everybody was going alongside the road, pulling two sticks. Not even the wheel, not even the wheel, in the 1970s. Okay.

We have the spiritual dilemma, then, of the animal instincts coming out of evolution—can't be avoided—so that's our karma. We have the karma of the animal kingdom, right? If you didn't have the karma of an animal kingdom, we'd all be in spirit; we wouldn't be sitting on our butts in chairs—we would be floating around the room, which I really like myself. I have never been an enthusiast of the human body. As a kid, other kids seemed to very enthused about it. They liked to wrestle and do all kinds of disgusting things—get their dirty, grimy fingers that they've been picking their nose with and stick it in your eye in a wrestling match. No, thank you! Disgusting! I never liked locker rooms. And anyway, the physicality of being an animal was never my greatest thing. While the other kids were playing hoop ball, I was reading the *Great Books of the Western World*.

That's how people enter the world. They enter at a certain thing. It comes out of their past experience, their past life, their past decisions. And apparently, there's a decision now to transcend the physicality and the compulsion of the animal. What we in spiritual work try to do is overcome the compulsiveness of the ego—of the animal reflex, to not automatically respond with guilt, automatically respond with fear. So, as we go up, we become more and more free.

Somewhere up here on the Map is the word *freedom*. I've lost it. Well, as you begin letting go of things, you come out of this level and you begin to reach a level called "neutrality." I'm starting out on the lower levels. And we'll move up; things will get better as we move along. I wanted to handle today's headlines. So, that's the animal mess. We can stop feeling guilty about animal impulses. We can forgive them. I think everybody should give their body a nickname and adopt it as a pet. I have adopted this body as a pet. And you see how friendly it is. It does what I want it to do. It expresses . . . I mean, it's a marvelous thing. It does all kinds of wondrous things. The best thing to do is to make a friend with it and get to know it for what it is. It wants to win. It wants to survive. It has all these animal needs, and we can stop feeling guilty about it. If you don't feel guilty about it, you don't have to deny it. If you don't deny it, I mean, what kind of animal are you, anyway? Don't you want to win? What are you, stupid? What? Of course, you want to win! If somebody passes you on the highway, don't you want to drive them off the highway and watch 'em turn over? Of course you do—it's fun! "There, take that, you . . . !" Okay, so you cheer your animal on; you become its champion. You see what's happened now? You adopted it. It doesn't have power over *you*. See, by owning it, you don't have to deny it. When you don't deny it, you don't have to feel guilt. When you accept it for what it is, you don't have to project it into the world. So, you don't see all that evil in the world anymore, because you stopped projecting it. Because you feel guilty about various things, you project it into the world. You think *they* are after *you*. That's your projection onto the world. The world then becomes a movie in which you see that which you project. The more you own the downside, the less you project. And now, instead of seeing the world as tragic, like my grandmother and crying all morning every time she read the paper, you see it as an absurdity. It's an absurdity.

So now as you move up levels, it becomes tragic but also absurd. Not to really be taken seriously. Why? Because each player on the field is where they are as a result of their own decision to be there. It's by one's own choices. Terrorists who blow up buildings make those choices consciously. They deliberated, made careful plans. Nobody forced them to do it, did they? Everyone here is here because we've all made choices, and I want everybody to become friendly with their ego—to accept their id, give it a name, become its owner, put it on a leash. That's the wisdom of the famous Zen ox-herding pictures, is it not? In the beginning, the ox is wild and untamable, and then with spiritual evolution, you see the person riding the ox.

Kinesiological Testing

When we test kinesiology, we ask for permission. The technique is very, very simple. It takes about 20 seconds to learn this technique. Let's ask a fun question: "The time of your death is already set at the time of your birth, resist." (True.) You don't have to worry about death anymore, and you don't have to worry about heaven. Aren't you glad? The moment you're going to leave is already preset, so there's no point worrying about death and worrying whether every bite of lasagna is going to kill you or not, because if you're destined to go at 82, whatever you eat is whatever you eat, you know what I mean? On the other hand, you might be in lousy health when you die instead of good health. Croak over in the pink, you know, I'd like to croak over in the pink. You know what I mean?

I don't think suicide is predestined, because that would mean we violate the freedom of the will of God. No, you would have the choice of life versus death. At that point, you have the choice of life or death or surrendering to God. So, the point of suicide is a critical spiritual opportunity. At that point one can completely surrender the totality of all you think you are and what is going . . . you can surrender all of it to God. You can either die from suicide, or suddenly go into a really high state. You can transcend right from the doors of hell. Heaven and hell are a tenth of an inch apart. And having been there, I can attest to the truth of that statement. From the very depths of hell, which are worse than anyone can imagine, there was the total surrendering and then emergence into a totally different paradigm.

To merely hear certain information already has a transformative effect, just the hearingness of the information. Just to know you don't have to fight your ego, blame it, feel guilt about it, go to hell because of it; you can adopt it as a pet and train it. You know, it's fun. You should champion all its animal instincts and say, "Hey, good for you, you did just what you were supposed to do." Instantly you're off the guilt, you understand what I'm saying? You're on top of it instead of underneath it.

Consciousness Calibration of Humanity

These levels of consciousness, then, are really the evolution of consciousness toward the light. It would be like, that is an innate quality of consciousness itself. On the other hand, consciousness is in no hurry. It can take eons; eons. "This consciousness . . . We have permission to ask about it." (True.) "Has existed for eons, resist." (True.) Before all-time even started, I am . . . was . . . have been. So, that which you are, it's already has been around for eons, understand? And out of all those eons, this is where it has arrived at, at this moment. And we can then calibrate that and even reflect it on this Scale of Consciousness. We have a pointer now. As I say, if you hold it in mind, it'll appear. I just realized that. That is funny, isn't it?

We said that society reflects this Map of Consciousness®. If we calibrate the level of consciousness of all of humanity, here's where it is: 78 percent is below 200. Consequently, what do you think today's newspaper is going to be about? It's going to be . . . because the newspapers are generally around 385. This is *CBS News*, NBC, the news broadcasts are around the upper 300s. The news also focuses a great deal on the 400s, and we'll be talking about the 400s later. That's the percentage—that's how the world population is distributed.

Distribution of the Levels of Consciousness of Mankind
©The Institute for Spiritual Research, Inc. dba Veritus Publishing

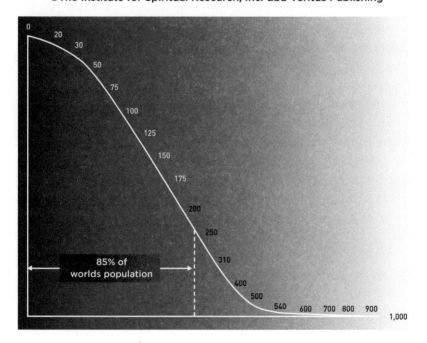

Eighty-four percent of the population transcends 10. That leaves 16 percent to die, right? Sixteen percent is in the process of death itself or very close to death. The United States of America calibrates in the 400s. The modern European, Western civilized world calibrates in the 400s. This is the world of civilization as we know it—civilization as we know it, how it has evolved until this point in time. That was just to give you an idea of distribution. The majority of mankind, when you see how that's distributed, you see that the majority of mankind has not reached the level of Integrity, around 200. The majority of mankind is in the lower part of the box, which gives you a certain degree of compassion for it. In other words, people can't help being other than how they are.

Whether someone is a perpetrator or a victim is all a point of view. Is Osama bin Laden a perpetrator? No. He's the victim of ignorance. Is he someone to hate or someone to feel sorry for? To be so ignorant about the nature of God and reality, to be so unevolved. Even the wolfpack cares for its mates. So, is he someone to be hated? So, we might say that people in the lower part of the box are the victims of their own ignorance. That's what Jesus said, when he said, "Forgive them, for they know not what they do." Their level of consciousness is not high enough for them to even see that they have got a choice to be other than they are.

So, one of the consequences of karma is the range of choice. People at the bottom of the box don't have the choice to be other than what they are. Spiritual evolution has been won, earned. To have a choice—that you have a spiritual option is a choice. See how few are the options of a person at the bottom of the box. If you're born on certain streets in certain big cities, you either become a member of the gang or you die, right? I always get a kick out of treatment centers. We take them out of the gangs, we treat them with all this, and you send them back. How are they going to survive? You want them to be like middle-class Protestant America's ideal on the streets of the inner city? Good luck. You want to survive, you have to transcend it. Why? Because then you have choices. You don't have any choices when you live on a certain block. You either join the gang that runs that block, or you get eliminated. You don't have the choices. To see that, then you see that each person is, to some degree, the victim of where they are in the evolution of consciousness. To some degree, if you like victimology—victimology is a very big subject in today's society. There's a great deal of competition to be victim. Everybody is trying to get into the camera.

We said that over here, the lower levels are force. And that force is a substitute for power. Those who have power don't need force, because they influence everything within their domain by virtue of what they are, by virtue of what one has become. *So, the greatest service we can give to all of humanity is to become all that we can become to the best of our ability.* And that energy radiates out and lifts the level of consciousness of all of mankind.

The Dangers of Righteousness

Mankind was at 190, 190. That's pridefulness, arrogance, and, of course, denial. That's the rule of righteousness. Righteousness scares me, because righteousness is the justification for every major devastation we've ever seen in society. When people talk about the righteous, give me a break! It is out of righteousness that all the horrors of mankind arise. Mankind's history, if you watch the History Channel, it is a fascinating channel to watch, because you see the evolution of consciousness as it expresses itself in the interactions of society in different cultures throughout all of time. When I was a kid, I hated history because it seemed like a dead subject, but now it's my favorite subject, because you see the dance of the ego as it expresses itself in human interaction. And you can calibrate the levels of the playing fields involved—and Napoleon and Henry VIII. When you calibrate all the levels of the monarchs throughout history and a great many other world leaders, you see why the world was the way it was.

It is only by becoming conscious that a person can avoid being swayed by the demagogues who routinely sway society. So, down here we have force, and force is a substitute for power. Over here, everybody is miserable. They're not deserving to live. The view of the self: miserable, undeserving of life, evil, tragic, frightening, disappointing, weak. Now, as we get up toward anger, one's self-view becomes belligerent. So, the kids we get off the street at the treatment center are belligerent. If you don't flag their colors as you go by, you've been dissed, and now that justifies stabbing them, or something. They live in a strange world, see, with its own rules. So, the viewpoint of God, then, is a reflection of one's level of consciousness. And this culturally, as it gets expressed over the centuries, has had a profound impact on society. Profound impact.

These are all levels of egomania, in a way. These are all levels of egocentricity. At the bottom of the box, God despises you. God hates you. He throws you into hell because you are a worthless, sinful worm. Because you're evil, you see God as vindictive. This is the God of the Old Testament. This is the God of the Old Testament. So, these are the negative depictions of God that come out of, as Freud said, out of the unconscious, out of the id. All that you hate and despise about yourself, you project onto a deity. The God of the Old Testament and many other cultures are really demonic. These are the demonic depictions of God. God despises you; he's vindictive; he's also sadistic. He likes to be cruel and throw you into hell for endless torture. He disdains you. He has nothing to do with you. He condemns you. He is punitive—God gets even with you. The God of the Old Testament was prone to jealousy and vanity, and he would get pissed and blow you away. Punitive God—so, this is the God of Judgment Day that everybody is scared of. Let's settle Judgment Day. We took care of death and heaven and all.

Judgment Day

Let's do Judgment Day. "We have permission to ask about Judgment Day, resist." (True.) "Judgment Day is today, resist." (True.) Thank you. Judgment Day is today. "Judgment Day for this person here is now, today." (True.) "For the persons in the audience is today, resist." (True.) Every day is Judgment Day because every day, you make a decision that moves you as an iron filing in the electromagnetic field of God. To be here today has already changed your karma, instantly. Right? You're a different iron filing than you were yesterday. Every day is Judgment Day. If you die right now, you're going to go wherever you are at, right this instant. Right? Next week, God's not going to change.

So, this God is punitive. The angry God. This God denies you. The person is always wanting something. These are the prayers: "Dear God, please give me a new Cadillac, a new Mercedes Benz." What's that song by Janis Joplin? So, this is where kids get disillusioned about religion and God, you know. I remember running to catch the bus. I lived out in the country and it was a mile to the nearest bus, and I had a violin lesson in town. I get out of school 5 minutes late, and the freaking bus leaves in 20 minutes. I've got exactly one mile to go and I'm running with my violin, and I'm praying up a storm. I mean, I was really pissed. If you missed your violin lesson and you missed the bus, God help you. And just as I got close to the bus, it drove away. Well, umm. That's what we all have to face sooner or later in childhood: "I pray to pass the test"— and you got a D-minus.

So, here God's angry, he's mad at people. God seems to hate people. I mean, if God's the creator of man and woman, why would he hate you? He created us as not having the ability to tell truth from falsehood. Life would have been different if Eve had known kinesiology. She had never attended one of my lectures, so . . . She gave in to curiosity. Out of that curiosity, then, she went from the oneness—the Garden of Eden is the peace and stillness of oneness—and she bought into duality. She bought into perception. And out of duality, you get conflict, good and evil, heaven and hell, and all the rest. So, she bit into what the 400s does best, and this from that. So from an enlightened state of innocent simplicity in which there is no conflict, there was the buying into the world of perception, and there was born duality. And thus, the fate of man is—allegorically, at least—described.

All right. So, these gods are very angry gods, and not only vengeful, but here's a god who's indifferent. Here I am, running for my violin lesson, and what the hell—am I nobody in the world? So, this is your view of yourself as a worm. You pray up a storm, and nothing happens. This is the disillusionment of childhood with religion. They prayed and prayed for something, and it never happened . . . so-and-so died anyway. Yeah. All right.

Courage: The Level of Empowerment

Now we get to Courage. Our view of God begins to change. God is perhaps a possibility and of a different nature now, because now 200 is a level of empowerment. You remember EST back in the '70s, Werner Erhard Seminars Training. The purpose of EST was to get you off projecting blame and to own—to become empowered by owning—that it wasn't the traffic that made you late. If you were late to an EST meeting, you had to stand outside the door, and the trainer would ask you why you were late. You would say, "Well, I missed the bus." You would have to stand there and wait some more. "And the elevator was slow." Uh-huh. "And the alarm didn't go off." Uh-huh. And finally he said, "I chose to be late." "Okay, you may come in now." You had to own yourself, that some aspect of you decided that, see. Some aspect. You didn't set two alarms, you didn't set a backup to make sure, et cetera. The reason Werner did that is because he tried to get you over the level of 200. If you did EST, you were successful if you now had the courage to own your own decisions and take responsibility.

Down here, the blame is put out there. These kids that I treat at the Girls Ranch, they never did anything wrong—the other one always made them do it. Many famous murderers, famous murderers that preoccupied the public for a long time—the reason that perpetrator never appears to be guilty is because "she deserved it." "She made me do it." "She made me do it; what's there to feel guilty about?" To not own. So, that person calibrates below 200. The difficulty with getting the kids in the Girls Ranch to improve is you can't get them to own that they're the author of their own decisions. So, here the blame is put out there; it's the other guy's fault.

So, you affirm, then, at 200 you have Courage. When you get up to 250 it's Neutrality; 250 is you become released from attachments. There's a method known as "releasing," which I think is a very excellent method—letting go of wanting to change things, to control things. You become detached, so you stop controlling everything and stop worrying what people . . . If you are a good releaser, you certainly end up at least at 250, which is Neutral. Neutral is very comfortable, people at Neutral. Here, if you don't get the job, you kill yourself or you kill the other guy, or you blame yourself—you go into a depression and stop eating and take an overdose.

Neutral

Up here in Neutral, it is okay if it goes that way, and it's okay if it doesn't. You're not riding on what happens out there. You're not living on the projections of the ego. In Neutral, if you get the job, it's okay, and if you don't, there are a lot of other ones. Anybody who tells me there is unemployment doesn't know what they're talking about. I can open the employment page—"Jobs Wanted," "Help Wanted" pages of any newspaper in the United States— and find three or four pages of jobs. I can walk down any street in America, and it says "Help Wanted" anywhere. They do it in Sedona. It's not "out there"—unemployment is not "out there." Unemployment is in your head. Right after World War II, the vets came back—we all got $52.20. I only got $52.20, but I also had three jobs at the same time.

Willingness

So, the Willingness, then. Neutral is okay. As we get up to Willingness, we have a whole different inspiration. God is inspiring, things look hopeful. People in Willingness are fun to be with. People in Willingness are cheerful, optimistic; they help. If one or two people are trying to lift a sofa, a person in Willingness comes over and says, "Can I help?" They just automatically do that. They do that because that's who they are; when you're moving up to Lovingness, you're becoming an asset on the planet. These people at lower levels are a detriment on the planet. In fact, the 78 percent below that level there, are really supported by these at the top. These are the people at the top that keep these lower-level people alive. If it wasn't for the people at the top, they wouldn't have sidewalks to walk on. You wouldn't have a car to get into. You wouldn't have the steel to make the car. These people are powerfully productive. So, the sales manager just gets the team together, he gives them a pep talk; they all feel fantastic when they walk out. It's because he is probably at least 350 or so. He's up there in the positive . . . These are the go-getters of the world. What gives them their power is intention. So, what Werner taught in EST, if it's your intention absolutely to get to that lecture at one o'clock, you will be there. And failure to be there at one o'clock is a defect of intention. Werner always made you responsible for your intention. It means your intention is out. Your integrity is out. If your intention is there, intention overcomes all kinds of obstacles.

And a fierce, determined intention can overcome almost anything in this world. Fierce intention is what you discover in sports, or in exercise, or in labor, when you reach the point beyond which you cannot go. You white-knuckle it, clench your teeth, and by your intention, you drive through the barrier. It's an incredible experience to do it. Many people have had it in sports and running and various ways. I discovered it in a warehouse when I could not lift one more box of canned goods in Wisconsin, out in 110 degrees in a pea cannery, in this warehouse with no windows. I could not lift one more box. Not one more. I was never a heavyweight to begin with. Anyway, after 12 or 14 hours in this heat and no water and God-knows-what-all, I said, "I can't do it." And then something came up, and there was this incredible decision to go through the barrier. I crashed through the barrier and all of a sudden, the boxes became weightless. I lifted them like feathers. I could have kept going for days. And I've done that many times when I am lifting stone, and all. Once you discover what is beyond that barrier—the runner discovers that; pushes itself to the limit and will not accept the limit, and by intention drives through it. And suddenly the runningness happens of its own.

To some degree this is also exactly the same as it is with spiritual work—when you get to a certain point and you cannot go any further, and suddenly you're out in the free and everything happens spontaneously. So, Willingness is also the open door to success. Willingness is powerful because the person here on the Map owns that it's their intention, owns taking responsibility; they are optimistic, they are willing, the world is hopeful, and God now becomes an inspiration.

Acceptance is even higher than that, because in Acceptance, now there's a willingness to forgive on a spiritual level. Acceptance is a more harmonious and more merciful way. Instead of condemning your ego as being the evil in you and all the rest—the devil and Satan and giving it all kinds of horrific names—if we accept it, we forgive the ego for being what it is. I mean, it grew up as an animal. What do you think it's going to do—algebra? The animal in you isn't going to do algebra. So, we transcend positionality to forgiveness and acceptance.

CHAPTER 2

THE POWER OF FORGIVENESS

We come into a merciful state of mind. If you are merciful toward your animal, then you are merciful toward other people's animal, huh. So, when somebody passes you on the highway, you say, "Good luck. I don't care if he gets in front of me." We're all going to arrive the same place, same time, anyway, which is the next stop-and-go light. We're all going to be sitting there at the red. So, let them get a car ahead. It makes no difference.

The way you get to be a soldier is . . . you take somebody who hasn't got anything and you offer him a gun. Now he's instantly a soldier; he's on your side, willing to kill for you. All it takes is to give the guy a gun. So that macho, then, is an openness, and it comes from the animal world.

We can transcend that; we can forgive it and say that that's what comes from the animal world. One thing a person has to learn is how to handle their testosterone, right? It's one of the challenges of adolescence. We transcend a thing when we accept it. We accept it when we forgive it, and we feel merciful toward our own ego and that of others. People cannot help but be the way they are. And all the hypothetical objections that they could be other than they were—the hypothetical has no reality. There's no reality in the hypothetical. You hear it used all the time in bureaucratic, political arguments; the hypothetical is always posed, and then the defendant is supposed to defend himself against the hypothetical.

Forgiveness, then, is very, very important. In spiritual work, this is a level we all struggle for with our egos; being merciful toward ourselves, harmonious with others, accepting of ourselves and others without condemning them. Here's where we get off condemnation of others; right and wrong; judgmentalism; and righteousness, which is the worst of all the ego prideful positions. We transcend, and as we do, we come into understanding and capacity to comprehend, and we reach this wonderful level called Reason.

Reason, in which we now . . . God becomes wisdom, life becomes meaningful—my life is meaningful, and so is yours, and so is all of society. Down here on the Map, it is seen as hopeless. Higher up it is seen as awful, sinful, or terrible—or frightening—but now we see it as meaningful. You get curious. So, in the 400s, you see great curiosity. Everybody thinks, well, the intellect is truly human—no; the intellect, as we see until we become enlightened, everything all the way up the scale is still a refinement of the animal. The base of the intellect is curiosity, wanting to know. "What's here? What is this for? What does this do? What does that mean on there—'Pepsi'? Why is it red and blue?" Curiosity. Where do you see curiosity arise in the evolution of consciousness? In the animal. The animal's survival depends on curiosity. It's always nosing around, sniffing this, sniffing that, looking here, looking there. I look out my window and watch our animals, and they're all going here, going here; sniff this, sniff that. So, the animal, then, is still with us, and it is dangerous, as Eve found out. The desire to know—curiosity. Eat the apple of the tree. She just had to know what the hell that was like, right? So, that was the animal—just couldn't stop sniffing, poking its nose in. The downside of the animal, then, is you get trapped in curiosity. We're not talking directly about enlightenment itself today, but we will later.

The Spiritual Sideshow

A person struggling for enlightenment, you have to watch curiosity as a trap. Sedona is full of people trapped by spiritual curiosity.

They are into every kind of New Age circus and sideshow. They get distracted for years, following all kinds of leftovers from ancient Mesopotamia, you know what I am saying, which is the spiritual sideshow running all the time—from psychic reading here to running the runes on you there, to casting the stones, to doing your numbers, to reading the sole of your foot, to reading your hand, to looking in your eyes, to pulling your ears, counting the vertebrae, counting your bumps, phrenology—I mean the whole deal. You can spend lifetimes. The esoteric, the fascination of the esoteric. So, it's a sideshow. You walk down the sideshow, the same thing— here's the acrobats blowing smoke out of their ears, with needles stuck in them, weighs 82 pounds. He hasn't moved in 14 years. The last time he ate was 1937. Oh, he must be divine!

So, if we are animals and the animal is curious, naturally I checked them all out too, didn't you? Anybody who failed to check it out? Oh, wow. You've got a lot more books to read. You have to read every guru . . . They have millions of followers, folks, so it's a big business.

So, for the person who is dedicated to enlightenment, however, that's a trap. You haven't got time. The Buddha said, "Waste no time." And in the book—one of the books, first one, I think, or the second one—I forget—the second one, I think—it opens with "Waste no time." You don't have time to check all that out. If you're devoted to reaching some degree of enlightenment, you don't have the time to check out the astral circus. It is amusement; it's intriguing. What's intriguing about it is that it comes from elsewhere. Anything that is invisible and comes from elsewhere must be divine. The difficulty is, it doesn't know the difference between religion and spirituality. It doesn't know the difference between the occult and spirituality. The downside of Sedona is, it doesn't know the difference between the occult and spirituality. The difficulty with the traditional world—especially of Europe—is, it doesn't know the difference between spirituality and religion. The Constitution of the United States, which calibrates at 700, clearly defines the difference between religion and spirituality. It says spirituality okay, but no establishment of religion, so our trust in God is spiritually integrous with the Constitution.

The interesting thing about the 400s is, there's a great increase in power, because you don't have to lift barrels in order to count them. In the lower levels, you had to lift all those barrels to count them. When the intellect is born, you go, "Four times two is eight." Thank you. You don't have to lift any of them; you've already got how many's there. Your control now of the world of form is enormous, because you can abstract. You can deal with the abstracts. Your computer, of course, has very advanced capacity to deal with symbols and abstract significance. The downside of the intellect, however, is quite sizable, because it's also prone to error. It thinks that because a thing exists, therefore it has a comparable representation in reality—which is not so at all. The downside of intellectualism, which we hear every night on television: everybody's got some intellectual scheme.

Anyway, the downside of the intellect, then, is that it thinks the hypothetical is real; deals with the hypothetical as though it was a reality and doesn't know its own limitations. So, the downside of the intellect—the upside, you might say, is science. The downside is the egotism of science. It doesn't know its own limits. There's nothing built within the intellect to tell it when it's out of its own field, because the intellect is perfect for dealing with the concrete, and it's good for dealing with abstractions of the concrete. A true scientist knows the limitation of science. You see people on television, there's always some pseudoscientist trying to disprove all spiritual concepts—out-of-body experiences, near-death experiences; there're professionals on there all the time. Their whole life is dedicated to disproving any reality of the nonphysical domain. Their stake is heavily into physicality. The joke is, it's the nonphysicality of their subjective consciousness that allows them to think that objective physicality is all there is to life. I mean, that's just the little paradox that I see, because that's an abstraction to think that. Anyway, the 400s, of course, is the world of the intellect, the world of modern science, civilization, the university, great books. The *Great Books of the Western World*, which I was very fortunate to have a set. I was doing writing, and I needed references. I went to the Sedona library; it was having a sale, and for $500 I picked up a complete set of 1932 University of Chicago *Great Books of the Western World* which I really prize, because it's the greatest thinking of which man has been capable of since the time of the ancient Greeks, and right down until . . . The last book is Freud. Anyway, I hope somebody writes some newer ones since Freud. As a kid that's what I loved: reading the encyclopedia. And I still, if I could have a simultaneous other lifetime, I would spend it reading the *Great Books of the Western World* because it's just beautiful, the capacity of the human mind to address certain very difficult issues. Of course, it doesn't solve them, because there wouldn't be any more volumes to it, right? The ego cannot go beyond itself, so a true scientist says to you when a spiritual argument comes up, "I don't know. That's beyond the realm of science." There's an honest man for you. It's beyond the realm of science. He doesn't try to prove that the experience of the Presence of God is due to a lesion in the parietal region of the brain. There's a guy on television, he's always getting near-death experiences and things like that, out-of-body experiences, and trying to prove they're due to some locus in the brain or something very interesting.

Calibrating a Genuine Out-of-Body Experience

Of course, the way you differentiate it is, you calibrate the level of consciousness before and after the experience. Before and after a spurious experience, the consciousness level remains the same. Before and after a true experience, it shows an enormous jump. Let me just ask in this case here: "The jump after the experience in the snowbank was over 50." (True.) "60." (True.) "80." "90." (True.) "100." (True.) "150." (True.) "160." (True.) "180." (True.) "200." (True.) "300." (Not true.) The jump in the snowbank of this entity here that almost froze to death at age 11 or 12—before the experience and after the experience—it had jumped 300 points after the experience. The Presence of God prevailed, you know, and I wrote about it in the book. Anyway, I got out of the snowbank and into the snow, and this was profound, unbelievable—you just melted into the Presence—that which is infinite, wordless, beyond all form, not different than what you are. Strangely, at age 12, that which I was experiencing was not different than the reality of any sense of I, but it was all nonverbal. I never explained it to anybody, never mentioned it to anybody. But that jumped it 300 points.

If you poke something in the parietal region of the brain and you are 410 when you started, after the surgery you will still be 410. So, that's how you can tell whether it's genuine or not genuine. How about the out-of-body experience? Let's see if that had an effect: "The out-of-body experience when I was sick in bed. I was six feet over the bed. That resulted in an elevation of consciousness, resist." (Not true.) No, it didn't, see. Out of body, as strange as it was, it was highly educational to be weightless in the middle of space; it was great. I mean, I'm all for it, but the person came back the same. It was just strange, indescribable. In those days, nobody ever heard about such things, and I never discussed it with anybody except my analyst. We both decided it was a toxic condition of the brain and it caused a projection of the body image into a seeingness out . . . well, we'll let it go at that. We'd never heard about it. Anyway, because the TV confuses the two, I just thought I would demonstrate. Before and after the out-of-body experience, which was quite surprising—it happened back in the '50s, and nobody was on TV about it in those days—it was the same. But the near-death experience was profound.

The residual of the near-death experience—which I never spoke about until I wrote about it in 1995 in that book *Power vs. Force*—the residual was a complete elimination of fear: fear of death. During World War II, I had no fear of death at all. Mines could be going off and minesweepers blowing up and people dying. I mean, I was interested in whether we had coffee this morning. The generator was out because the electromagnetic tail took all the power, so there was no coffee. Well, that was the tragedy of the day: no coffee—not that you were going to get blown up. But you can't do that intellectually. If it happens, it happens of its own, so you can't say, "Gee, look at me, I am fearless," because it was just a side effect of that phenomenon. People who have had heart attacks and survived and near-death experiences, that's very common; the fear of death disappears. So, there's a transformation of consciousness.

Reason accomplishes a great deal. This is the world of theology: going to a theological university, you study about God and reason and comparative religion, and it's all very fascinating. Now we are going to go from there. This is a sudden movement of reverence and lovingness in which your view of yourself and others is benign. And it's sort of a falling in love . . . it happens to almost everybody spontaneously. You'll be walking along in the woods, and some little dog walks along. All of a sudden, you feel like a sense of delight. Unplanned moment out of nowhere. You were worrying about paying the rent, and all of a sudden, here's a sense of joyfulness. A dog, a dog's wagging tail. Let's do it: "That little white dog, his wagging tail is over 500, resist." (True.) That little white dog just charmed us. We were in a small town, and this workman's dog—a cute, little white dog jumps out of the back of his truck and comes over, and he just loved you up like crazy. And he wanted you to love him up. It was a 500 experience. I said, "Can a dog be 500?" Yes, by God, a dog can be 500. A dog's wagging tail is 500. And as I also say every lecture, a kitty's purr is also 500.

When we talk about the animal brain below 200, how does that fit? Is that just the observing consciousness, the wagging dog and kitty? I'm just speaking of it as an anatomical structure which arose through the animal world. However, it can be used for divine purposes. By the time you reach the evolution of the human, what was originally designed just as a dagger, or as something that can be used, so intention and purpose now begin to change the use of this complex machine—just like your computer can be used to watch movies on the Internet or it can be used to do research on the most advanced subjects. So now this animal brain, which is the substrate of the physicality of what goes on in our skulls, by intention it can be made to serve higher purposes and lead to spiritual evolution.

Of course, the kitty's not always at 200. Kitty's not always at 200 any more than the dog is always at 500. But neither is the human being. So, for some peculiar reason, there's some karmic and probably very interesting and entertaining reason behind this, which, as I say, if we had more years and time to check out why is it that the animal—and this particular animal—is capable of love, and why is *this* animal capable of love. We know that herbivorous animals in general tend to be lovable, but the canine and the cat are also carnivores, so here we have two carnivores that have the capability of lovingness. Lovingness. We all know how a cat goes for lovingness, and our cat is very attracted to lovingness, and loves people when they come into the house, and if they like kitties, instantly it's a match. So, here we have this reflection of human love coming up in animals that are more capable of love than 78 percent of the human population. That gorilla, Koko, calibrates over 240. Koko's famous, and she is frequently on the public-education channels. And Koko's learned a great deal about humans and has a lot of human motivations—seemingly human motivations—particularly in love, and is able to think and reason and use sign language. And interestingly can construct a sentence. Koko can actually construct a sentence and communicate with humans. I don't know the reason for that. But you're safer with Koko than with 78 percent of the people on the planet. Seventy-eight percent of people on the planet will steal you blind, but Koko knows that is your hamburger and will sit back and wait, because that's your hamburger.

Intention and Spiritual Will

The level of consciousness is set by karmic, apparently by karmic merit, which is the totality, the composite of spiritual decisions of the spiritual will. It's the spiritual will that is the source of the center from which you evolve spiritually. The center out of which you come for your spiritual work is the spiritual will. It's the spiritual will which sets karma, and not necessarily actions. "That is correct, resist." (True.) That is correct. The spiritual will. So, you see your feelings and your emotions shift up and down the scale here all the time, but that doesn't change your intention. Your intention is quite a deliberate thing. Your intention is more or less the stabilizer of the ship. And you make little corrections, you know, when you're driving. You are making constant little corrections in the wheel. But if your intention is to drive east, you will continue to drive east. These are fluctuations. We all periodically get annoyed, angry, fearful, et cetera, but our intention remains the same, so intention—a decision of the spiritual will is apparently what sets karma. When you have had a chance to think about it, reflect on it, and decide to make that move, then now that is permanent. So, every action, thought, feeling, every decision we make is then reflected in the infinite field of consciousness, where it is retrievable forever.

The reason kinesiology works is, we can go back and get what was the level of consciousness of Napoleon. We find out that many world leaders, including spiritual great gurus, et cetera, calibrate higher in the beginning of their careers than later. This is true of Napoleon, who was about 450 in the beginning. And then after a while, they get pulled down by the ego—greed and power over others, and selfishness and arrogance. So, Napoleon didn't stay 450: "Before he died, Napoleon was over 200, resist." (True.) "He was over 240." (Not true.) Napoleon had dropped about 300 points in the calibrated levels of consciousness. We see this also in very famous gurus who gained great millions of followers and world fame, et cetera. In the beginning of their careers, they usually calibrate in the 500s. They write books that are famous, et cetera. And then you say, "What is the level of this writing?" It is 500. "What's the level of this writer now?" Sometimes it is under 200. I was shocked. People with great names—and everybody would go "ooh" and "aah" when you mention their name—would calibrate in the low 200s; some even below 200.

So, that means that you can choose to go up or you can choose to go down. Oh. You can choose to go up or choose to go down. So, as Napoleon . . . Hitler, I think, was higher than he ended up. Where was Hitler when he wrote *Mein Kampf*? (1925). "Adolph

Hitler, we have permission, resist." (True.) "Was over 200 when he wrote *Mein Kampf*: 250." (Not true.) "He was over 245." (True.) "250." (Not true.) So, he was into nationalism, 250 when he wrote *Mein Kampf*. He was imprisoned at the time for a failed putsch, as I remember. Hitler, before he died . . . "We have permission, resist." (True.) "Before he died, he was over 60." (Not true.) All right. So, the spiritual will. He had many, many times to change his mind. But the reaffirmation of that direction apparently is what sets the karma.

So, the karma is like a little traveling program, a little computer chip in your spirit body; and it pretty much determines where you're going to go and how you're going to behave and what's going to happen. Is that predestination? Well, predestination is just a term. You could call it that; you could say that what befalls you in this lifetime is a combination of karma plus your exercise of the freedom of choice. On the other hand, karma has limited your choices. You cannot decide right now to become a squirrel in the next instant, you know what I mean? Your choices are limited. You can decide to be poor in a hurry, but to be rich in a hurry takes longer. Revelation. All right.

So, 500 is the beginning of a revelation that there's something more to life than just this stuff down here on the Map. You see, although the world is described in terms of the Newtonian paradigm of reality and the lower levels of the ego, life is lived in the subjective experience, which is indefinable. That which is experiencing that you are here now listening to the words—you don't even have to pay any attention to the words, what they're saying—to heck with it. You're still aware that you're here, right? So, one is innately aware of one's existence and what is being registered in consciousness, and that's where we live. That's where we live. When you get a new car, the thrill, the excitement is experienced subjectively. There's nothing objective out there. The car's not happy. There's some inner indefinable, and it's beyond form. Form may trigger the experience, in the form of a car or winning the lottery. That may trigger it, but *all* experience is subjective. The only reality there is, is subjectivity. That is the essence of *Eye of the I*, and the book which l am finishing now, called *I,* is that the Presence of God is found through absolute subjectivity—radical subjectivity.

Split Consciousnesses and Personalities

Can someone have a split consciousness? That brings up a whole different subject. It brings up the question of possession, and more than one personality in one body, and multiple personality disorder. It brings up the fact that entities of different realms can forcefully sometimes take over the consciousness of the human being. A human being can focus, and by karmic propensity, probably some karmic event, allow for, let's say, some lower astral to take temporary possession of the body and possession of your consciousness. So, you think things are happening that are really going on in a different domain, crossing over from one domain to another.

We had an entity coming up from another country, very insistent—sent all kinds of faxes. We would answer the faxes. Some of the faxes would be sensible, and then faxes would come through that were really stupid. I said, "We already answered that." This person insisted on coming all the way from Australia to see me, and we refused. We said, "No, we can't do that." Anyway, this entity was on the one hand well-meaning, calibrating in the 300s. And then a week later, a completely ridiculous fax would come through. That entity calibrated very low: 70. Both in the same body. Sometimes this guy would be really nice, doing everything for the good of mankind; the next thing, he was—he had really an evil intent about his visit to me. And I was very happy that he didn't get to meet me, or I might not even be here.

So, yes, there's a possibility, and it's a karmic inheritance. So, there are very negative spiritual decisions you can make that will then open the later karmic possibility for that which you just called in to visit you. You curse somebody to hell; now you get to see what hell's like. Some of the patients we see in the hospitals that are calibrating like 35 are doing so because of past serious spiritual errors. That may correctly agree with some religion, to some degree—that there are some things for which the Holy Spirit cannot forgive you. You'll have to work out the karma of that yourself.

Choice

Is there anything beyond choice? This question is really one of levels of consciousness. At a certain level of consciousness, choice is quite possible. It's more hypothetical than real, but it is also real. There're certain levels where choice is not possible. In the highest realms, no choice is going on. Everything is happening of its own as an expression of what in Sanskrit is called the *Purusha*, the Presence of God within as Self, which is manifesting through the human physicality as, let's say, this speakingness; this speakingness. There's no choice involved in this speakingness. It happens of its own. So, there are varying levels. As we go up the higher levels of consciousness, we'll get to that.

So, Forgiveness, Acceptance, Reason—you come up to Lovingness, which is the realm of most interest to spiritual people. Spiritual people are worried about how to get over the ego, how to get over the guilt of the ego, et cetera, and despair over it; and how to get to Love. Love is at 500 and is a whole different domain. Love is really the dawning of the light of the Presence of God within human consciousness in the nonlinear domain. At 500, you're well beyond the Newtonian. The Newtonian really reigns up through Reason. At 500, there's a different . . . the nonlinear begins to take precedence. It's Lovingness that makes the decisions, that's the background of your decision, lights up your decisions. And most people in spiritual communities, spiritual work groups such as this and others, are committed to reaching 540, is Unconditional Love. That's the saint—the saint is actually 575, but Unconditional Love calibrates at 540. That's what we all strive for. Most people in spiritual work strive first for Love and are delighted with it; then the energy of that Love leads them to drive on, and they despair over any limitation. That's the spiritual dilemma of the United States, our citizens, and how to handle global affairs. And you saw the endless discussions of ethics and morality, and certainly the United States has become reawakened to the seriousness of morality and what is ethical.

What's the ethical, spiritual, and what is the right way to handle this? The president, being Christian, then expresses Christian values. What is the position? What has the position of the church been? I forget who it was who talked about justified war. When is war justified? So, in the 500s, then, you have the whole dilemma. Down below, it's no problem. Up on the Map, there's the confusion of Christ saying, "Turn the other cheek." You get the sort of liberal wing, which says, well, you know . . . passivity. No, Jesus said—when he said to turn the other cheek, what he also said spiritually, and he also said, "Render unto God that which is God's, and unto Caesar that which is Caesar's." So, what he's saying is, "Don't mix levels." Even the indigenous tribes are very aware of this. They pray and pray and ask the animal for forgiveness. They love him, and he appreciates this love as they kill him. The indigenous understand the different levels. There's the physical level where, "Without this, I cannot live, and you are sacrificing your life for me, for which I give thanks to the Great Spirit." A sanctification of life. So, intention then is what sets the karma.

Love, Illumination, and Bliss

Unconditional Love, then, is the capacity to be in love—it's really "in love with life." You're driving along and all of a sudden, you feel a surge of joy. You're just sort of in love with life itself. And at 540 you pretty much fall in love with everybody, and people who belong to 12-step organizations know what that's like. You leave judgmentalism at the door, and everyone is unconditionally loving to the best of their ability. It leads to a saintliness, saintliness, and it brings you into Serenity, Joyfulness, a feeling of completion—and God is Infinite Love. The joy of life is that the Source of that life is the Love of God. That takes you into sort of an exquisite state, which is transfiguring. 540 is transfiguring. Your inner life is one of serenity. Although your emotions may jump around, they're not who you are, because the persona, the personality which interacts with the world is not who you are; and along the way with spiritual work, you realize that it's not what you are anyway—why are you wasting time with it? It doesn't need anything, and you could drop it anytime; you know what I am saying. "Why don't you drop that?" "Yeah, okay." So, it's not who you are, because if it's who you are, you're not going to drop it no matter what, because that's intention. But emotionality can come and go and doesn't need anything. Even a saint can get annoyed with something. It doesn't mean he's not saintly, but if you ask him if he believes that, he doesn't believe that. It's just the animal talking.

Illumination and Bliss at 600: there's a transformation which occurs with the surrendering all sense of self as the ego. So, 600 is the crossover from "I" as limitation and form to "I" as the field, as consciousness itself as the subjective sense of "I." The sense of "I" is coming out of an infinite, nonpersonal "I" which, as it comes through you, you personalize and give it a discrete "me-ness," but that's late in the process of Awareness. The one thing we are unanimous on is that you "are." The only thing you can say with absolute certainty is that you "are." And even at about 840, you're going to have to let that one go, and now you know whether you "are" or "are not," because that again becomes an abstraction. "To be" or "not be" is already again an absurdity to be let go of at 840.

So, now we've pretty much described the world—you know, a circus, a game, game board—the ego is an endless game board, and your TV is your latest tune-in on the game board of the ego as it plays out there. And what originated as the animal world has now been infused with spirit, and you see the ego playing itself out. So, the news is no longer depressing, any more than your little animal is depressing. He's a good fellow. My body has done everything I have asked him this morning. What more could you ask, huh? So, you make friends with your little animal, stop being angry at it, forgive it, adopt it, take responsibility for it, cheer it on. Cheer it on—life as a human being is extremely difficult. Jesus Christ said the same thing. You're between the physicality, the instinctual world of the animal, and the knowingness of the spiritual domain. That is a very purgatorial, almost, way. There's not just heaven, hell, and earth but an enormous, infinite number of possibilities on all levels of existence.

A lot of choices are really decisions, decisions. Choices come and go, but decisions are more long-lasting. Like the person said, "I couldn't decide whether to go to a movie or commit suicide." The option to see life as absurd is always there. To see it as comical is always there. To see it as sad and tragic is always there. The ego, of course, gets great benefit from choosing the lower positions, you know. The ego can't hang out too long if it starts picking up there all the time. So, it likes to get into self-pity and get on Channel 15 and sob. And you can juice that for a lifetime, you know what I mean? Pick a tragedy and mull on it and pull you off of it. The ego gets great satisfactions out of these lower things.

The Nature of the Ego

Seeing as how you are interested in spiritual evolution, how do you get out of this? There's more than just choice. It's understanding the nature of the ego. The ego gets enormous gain out of the bottom of the chart. There's nothing better than self-pity, nurturing hatreds, nurturing anger, nurturing a lifetime of injustices. If you lack an injustice, you can look back at your ancestors and find somebody who persecuted them, and you can get into that one. Everybody comes from somewhere back in time. And somewhere back in time, the Goths invaded you or the Anglos or the Saxons or the Normans. You know what I mean? You can always get revenge from somebody and adopt a political position and get banners and raise money from the government. You know what I mean. You can always get it by—so, even if you lack tragedies in your life, I'm sure if we look into your ethnic background, we'll find tragedies. And so, justification for a positionality is one of the jobs of the mind to perpetuate its existence. The ego is self-perpetuating, and it gets its energy out of the way it juices the lower positions.

You'd say, "Why would 78 percent of people want to stay in a nonintegrous position in life? First of all, they don't know what's integrous. As far as they're concerned, it is integrous. Killing your enemies is heroic, right? So, ignorance prevails over the whole field, but the payoff that people get out of these ego positions is what gives them their energy.

So, we've pretty much covered the course of the Map. Most people here are familiar with it. It's in the book *Power vs. Force*, it's in *Eye of the I*, and we'll reprint it again in *I*. The interesting thing was that consciousness . . . First of all, humans cannot tell the difference between truth and falsehood. This certainly gives that which is fallacious a tremendous edge. Between the yearning of the ego for something to juice, and not knowing the difference between truth and falsehood, you wonder that mankind got as far as it did. Finally, in 1986 it crossed over for karmic reasons. When we asked why that was so, it said the collective karma of mankind had justified it. So, the spiritual work of people that was being done at times of real, great darkness manifested as an advancement in the level of consciousness of all of mankind from which we all benefit. Our spiritual work constantly benefits others even if it's not a conscious intention, but that's the nature of consciousness.

God and Miracles

In the left-hand column on the Map, we put the View of God and, as you see, God goes from the despicable, really the lower-astral realms—we're talking about those energies that prevail in the lower-astral domains—and going all the way up to God as Infinite Love. As you move up, you move to a God that becomes progressively more experiential. In the 400s, God is a verbalization, an abstraction, a definition, and it depends heavily on concepts drawn from history, primarily religion. Religious history is one thing; enlightenment is another. What happens in the beginning is, a great Avatar appears. The Avatar calibrates at 1000, until at least recent times. A 1000 was the highest spiritual energy the human nervous system could handle. Even on the way up to 1000, it is often very painful, agonizing, and extremely difficult. The energy as you go up to 600 becomes exquisite. In the high 500s, the kundalini energy runs up your spine. It's exquisite. It's like an exquisite sensation, and it runs up your back, and up the spine and into the brain. If you think of the left side of the brain . . . you can run it to one side of the brain or the other, and it is exquisite. It goes on for . . . I don't remember how long it went on . . . a couple of years, I guess. Then it comes down, and it would come out the heart—heart region—and was also exquisite: exquisitely pleasurable, indefinably exquisite. On occasion it would go somewhere; this energy would, of its own.

That's the time of the miraculous, also. That's the time . . . that was the time of the miraculous and many of the so-called—what they're called, *siddhis*. They come about as a result of the energy field, which exists on its own. The miraculous happens within the field, as a result of the field. It has nothing to do with you or a person.

We were sitting in a restaurant in Korea, and somebody said to me, "This is a lady we brought to see you." This lady sat down and explained that one side of her brain had gone dead and was paralyzed. And then she stopped talking, and she went away, and everybody marveled at that. We got endless letters that this woman had become cured. Cured by the energy? Then there was a period of years when that would happen all the time. People would sit down and have all kinds of things and walk away fine. It's the energy doing that. The energy has the capacity to do that. There's no decision on anybody's part. It's probably a karmic potentiality arises and brings the person into the field, and the field happens of its own. *A Course in Miracles* says the same thing. It's by virtue of the Holy Spirit that the transformation comes about as a result of the Self with a capital *S* within the other, within the aura of that Presence.

So, up to 600 the subjective experience is one of increasing joy, radiance, effortlessness; everything happens by synchronicity. If you think, "I forgot a pointer," a pointer suddenly appears in the world. And that's normal. That's what life is like when it's normal. It's because of the harmony; everything is in synchronicity and things are not disconnected in time. There is the point where there is not a "this" causing a "that"; there is a unity that from perception looks like a "this" and "that," but it's all a unity. So, as you think, *Salt*, the waitress says, "Would you like some salt?" And it all happens of its own.

Transcending Causality

To see how this comes about, you have to transcend causality, the ordinary understanding of causality, which we did in the first lecture. There is no "this" causing a "that." Everything is coming about as a fulfillment of its destiny as set by the qualities inherent in its essence, because creation is continuous at all times. So, you don't see a "this" causing a "that." What you see is creation unfolding thusly. And, as the electron on this side of the universe spins this way and this one is in concert, it's not that this electron is causing this one to react, but that which is unfoldingness as the simultaneity of the two, which was expressed by Carl Jung as "synchronicity." So, there is no "this" causing a "that." The field brings about the potentiality within the field. The higher the field gets, the greater is its capacity to do that. As an electromagnetic field gets stronger and stronger, it can lift heavier and heavier particles of metal, you know.

The Ultimate Source is the Unmanifest. The Ultimate Source is the Unmanifest, beyond all universes. There's an infinite number of universes, infinite number of planes, infinite number of domains, infinite number of dimensions; all coming out of the Unmanifest. As the Unmanifest becomes manifest, inherent within the manifest is the quality of creation. There's not a "this God" causing a "that thing." Creation, then—the power of Creation is that which accounts for your existence. The evidence for the Presence of God is your own existence, because nothing of its own has the power within it to create its own existence. To account for that, for not seeing that, the ego thinks there's an endless string of billiard balls in a string called "causality." God started the first billiard ball going, and now evolution has gone, and then, after you leave this physical domain, God's waiting at the end.

That which is infinite Power, then, manifests as what we experience as existence. That Godness—I mean, that's what we call God—God is the infinite potentiality that can manifest as creation, as the universe, as all the universes, and all the universes. To experience that that is the Source of one's existence, that one *is* that which brings forth, then is called enlightened.

The Higher Levels of Enlightenment

On the way up to 600, then, the journey is increasingly exquisite. In the high 500s, life becomes synchronous. One sees only love everywhere. One sees only beauty everywhere. Nothing else seems to exist. There's a period that you go through where you can't stop crying. In spiritual traditions, this is well recognized in certain monasteries. Anyway, as you get into the high 500s, there's a sensitivity to the presence of love. You're in an airport and a man looks at his wife with a loving glance, and instantly you cry. It's just too much; you can't handle it. And that's one reason I don't talk about the way to God through the heart until later in my lectures. Otherwise, this would consist of one lecture, because as that energy comes up, it's almost incapacitating. Prior to that, there are periods of high energy, of exquisite joy. Periods of the happening of what the world calls "miraculous." There's less and less awareness of the physical body; you can forget it even exists and be surprised when you see it passing a mirror. I can remember wondering, *Who's in the house?* That was the mirror. And one time I tried walking through a wall, and bang! The physical body was still in this domain. The nose got a little flatter, though!

So, transcending identification with the body. So, first we transcend identification with the body as "I"; eventually the feelings as "I"; the thoughts as "I"; and the infinite state even beyond consciousness. That Which I Am is beyond Consciousness itself. It's That out of which Consciousness arises, out of which

Consciousness arises. That which is non-form is present in all form. It is out of the Formless that form arises.

So, the journey to the 600s is exquisite. Making friends with your ego is the best thing to do. Learn to pet it, like it, love it, forgive it, because on the way, you go through these extraordinary states. The presence of the not-paranormal—what would you call it? I don't know what it was. Things would happen even within the physical domain merely by imagining it. Electronic equipment especially would fix itself, just like that! To this day, I can't hold certain thoughts in mind without the electric in the car going out. Somebody asks me to look at something negative, it can blow a fuse! So, there is some kind of a connection between the physical and spiritual.

Then, out of the high energy coming out of the heart, near the high 500s, there is a state of exquisite bliss. There's a state in which all is wiped out and the mind becomes silent. And one becomes immobilized. At 600 the mind stops, is silent, is only the Infinite Presence of That which you are, beyond all time, beyond all dimension, and yet, not different from that which Is; all one and the same thing. The Divinity of existence shines forth through all that exists. That's why it is hard to function, because all reflects Divinity, no matter what its form. So, in that state, incapacitation occurs. No function is possible. Whether the body survives or not depends on karma and that which is around you. If the karmic propensity is for the physicality to survive, then the requirements to make that happen are there. To this day, the body doesn't eat unless somebody reminds it half the time, and were it not for very good friends, the body would be thinner than it is; so, somebody reminds you to eat.

Beyond 600—usually everyone stops there—are those who become enlightened. At 600, about half the people will not survive. Half of the people will leave the world, because you don't have to stay in the world. So, the option to leave is available. From the high 500s, from 600 up, there's no necessity to hang onto the body; this is strictly an option. You can leave anytime you want. To make it happen, all you have to do is picture yourself as leaving the body, and it happens. Then some karmic propensity from some higher level will prevail. We went up to 600; that goes from 700 to 1000. Beyond 600, I'm not sure how one survives it, really. The change is profound. Everything becomes silent, and in the silence, everything stands forth in exquisite brilliance; shines forth as brilliance.

Consciousness usually stops there, doesn't go further. First of all, there's no "further" to go. One has already become the ultimate possibility. There is nothing and nowhere to go from there, so it would not come to anybody as an option. In that state, there is nothing beyond that state, because that state is what one has always been prior to what the world calls "time." That which occurred in the snowbank at age 12 was already the Infinite Presence as Self, beyond all time, and the understanding That Which I Am existed before this universe or any universe was already a knowingness. All this is nonverbalized, so the spiritual information from the high 500s on up never comes about as thinkingness. It isn't that you think "this" and therefore you then reach "that," because it's nonlinear. It's more like a presentation and awareness that—like when you get up in the morning and realize it's light out. Nothing you did caused the light—the light just comes up of its own and illuminates all that is. So, we never went beyond the 600s in our calibrated scale.

The light of Divinity really shines forth now at what we say is the level into 500, where the opening of the heart now differentiates people from those that are loving and those that are less than loving but still positively oriented. At 540, it becomes unconditional. The purification continues, and then at 600 is this enormous transformation which cannot really be described. Generally, it stops at 600, and statistically we found that 50 percent leave the world there, and 50 percent stay.

Now, those that stay, what happens to them? It's not of any statistical significance to the world, because the number of individuals is small. It's of importance only to the impact it has on the world. At 600, one is blissed-out—Satchitananda. You can't give a lecture on spiritual things without using a few Sanskrit terms. Can't talk about joy and bliss without mentioning Satchitananda.

Calibrated Scale of Consciousness:
The Enlightened and Divine States
© The Institute for Spiritual Research, Inc. dba Veritas Publishing

The Supreme Godhead-God Unmanifest	∞
God Manifest as Divinity/Creator	∞
Archangel	50,000+
"I" as Essence of Creation	1,250
"I" of Ultimate Reality	1,000+
Christ, Buddhahood, Krishna, Brahman	1,000+
Avatar	985
God (Self) as Logos	840
Self as Beyond Existence or Non-Existence	800
Teacher of Enlightenment*	750
"I"/Self-Divinity as Allness (Beatific, Vision)	700
Sage-Self as God Manifest	700
Self as Existence	680
"I Am"	650
Enlightenment	600
Sainthood – Sat Chit Ananda	575
Unconditional Love	540
Love	500

From those who've traditionally been called enlightened, from the Avatar through the Saint—so, here's the Avatar: Christ, Buddha, Krishna, Brahman; different names in different cultures. That consciousness, at 985—a person at 985 has the capacity to send forth and radiate into the world an energy field where it tends to recontextualize reality of all of mankind for centuries. What happened 2,000 years ago defines right through the next 2,000 years and 2,000 years and 2,000 years—our definitions of right and wrong, value, the 10 Commandments, the courts, the judiciary; its influence of architecture, values, mores, human behavior's profound, even without being stated. So, it's the power of that energy field which contextualizes the consciousness of all of mankind. So, the value, then, is not specifically the specifics of a teaching, but the fact that an energy field at 1000 appeared within the consciousness of mankind, thereby transforming it, because power is a reflection of context. A context at 1000 has sufficient power to influence all of mankind throughout all of time. That power and that consciousness is still present. Although the entity that came and left—and reflected it to us—has come and gone, the energy remains, the energy remains.

In the high 500s, we went from Love to Unconditional Love. At 575, we say those people are saintly. This is what people, the naive spiritual seekers—at least in the beginning—think they're going to find. They're going to find somebody who is saintly walking around in sandals, with long hair, a staff, and a robe, who smiles sweetly at you. At that point, the sound of gongs is heard. "Ohm" is heard in the background. Incense arises in the air. Well, it doesn't happen that way necessarily. If you know Zen masters, you know you're more likely to get bonked over the head: "Wake up!"

Anyway, sainthood may take different forms, but when it first hits you, this is how it hits you. So, you're not going to keep your job at XYZ Corporation for very long, sitting there blissed-out in front of the computer, and you have accomplished nothing since this morning at eight. Nor have you moved or gone for lunch, and people begin to speak of you that "He is maybe a little, you know, touched." At that point, most people leave the world. You leave the world, especially a complex world like New York City, and you come to a smaller place, very often, where other people are spiritually oriented, and your condition is permissible. It is permissible to walk around blissed-out in Sedona . . . It used to be; I don't know if it is anymore. It would probably get you a ticket now. But when I first came here, you could walk around blissed-out, and people would say, "Man, he's just blissed-out." Which means you didn't need to change your clothes, didn't have to eat; you could get skinny, you never bothered getting a haircut, your beard got longer and longer, and you were just blissed-out, and it was okay. It was fine. "Hey, don't you think you ought to eat something?" . . . your friends would say to you.

So that was a community, a safe community. Therefore you often see a shift of community. People will leave a complex, demanding . . . because it's so much in form. What happens at 600 is that the world of form is very, I don't know, very difficult. It's very difficult to think of form; it takes energy, like understanding, comprehending in a languaging way what people are talking about. It takes energy. You have to keep saying, "What?" And the meaningfulness of it comes to you from a different domain, so there's a translation of form into non-form so that one is aware of what favorite fish you are talking about. Anyway, fish and I understand each other. The nonverbal communication becomes progressively important. That's why the communication with animals becomes very easy. You and the animal know exactly where you're at with each other, and nothing need be said. Your intention is read in an instant by that animal, and you can read its intention and come back to it with what it needs to calm it. And the snake will lay there. The snake will coil up and start to strike, and then this profound stillness and peace prevails. It dominates the snake; the snake cannot strike out of that field, because it's a perfect field of peace and safety, and it's more powerful than the snake. The snake is just entranced with you, and it sits there and looks at you for minutes. It's never seen a human being before, and he's just walked away from it, you know. And finally he goes away by himself and says good-bye and rattles his tail. And all is safe in peace, because that is the domain which is prevailing.

So, at 600, then, very often it's not possible to function, and those of you that are into serious spiritual work, it's probably advisable to have somebody that knows you [and] that knows you have done serious spiritual work, because you can be thought of as catatonic and taken away to a hospital. That happened one time on a rock, and there was nothing that would get the body off the rock at all. It was just blissed-out, and no threat, no thought— "Take him away, give him a shock treatment, give him Thorazine, put him in a mental hospital"—it didn't matter; "Arrest him," nothing. Nothing got him off the rock except love. The love for something that was about to happen got the body off the rock. So, love alone had the power to do that. So, I would say—because you can make sudden jumps, sudden leaps in consciousness, and you will not know they are coming . . . You can be sitting there chanting and doing some releasing system or technique or something, and you do this every day for two hours a day—I meditated for that—and nothing seems to be happening, and suddenly walk down the street and find yourself in a totally different universe. So, it's good that friends of yours know that you are not catatonic, and if you have a silly grin on your face and get faint at the sight of love, maybe they should just make sure you eat and look after you. So, 600—many people, as they get close to that, they seek out spiritual communities, they join ashrams, move to a place like Sedona—or at least the way Sedona used to be—where such states are understood and intuited, and people can tell when people are in sort of a blissful state.

The awareness, then, at 600 is when "am-ness" never came as an awareness. At age three, that which I've described before, I came out of oblivion, came out of the Void—the belief in the Void of previous Hinayana Buddhist lifetimes that the ultimate reality was Void. I was Void. The misunderstanding of Void as nothingness, which is a very serious spiritual error that's made in the Buddhist tradition—there're serious errors in the Christian tradition—the Buddhist tradition is not understanding the Buddha's teaching about Voidness. That which is nothing—you know, *no-thing*—is not the same as nothingness. Nothingness cannot exist as a reality, because for it to be, it would already have to exist, which voids it already as a . . . you know what I am saying? Besides, there would be nobody to be there to talk about it, so there would be no speaking of Void. What would tell you the ultimate reality is Void? It just disappeared, right? No, because no-thingness. That was the presentation at age three or four, was out of nothingness, because previous lifetimes due to that belief system, and I was a very arduous Buddhist monk, Hinayana Buddhist monk—went out of body—Void. That's a belief system.

The ego's belief in Void can manifest Voidness as a subjective experience. However, it's not the ultimate reality, or you would stay there. You don't stay there, because it's not the ultimate reality. Oblivion is a belief system. Voidness would happen. There were lifetimes in which that did *not* happen, and there is a lineage between the lifetimes. But this lifetime came out of Voidness again, and wham! There was this body in a little wooden wagon, and it was spring and the warm sunlight going on. Of course, this three-year-old doesn't know how to talk yet; doesn't know words or anything. And is stunned with the shocking fact of existence. And with the shocking fact of existence instantly arose the fear of nonexistence. Its corollary, its opposite came up. That calibrates at 940. I think existence versus nonexistence, 840. So, this was what the three-year-old was already looking at—that conflict: polarity, a very advanced spiritual dilemma of existence versus nonexistence. Was the ultimate reality existence or nonexistence? Is it one or the other, or neither, you know? In the nonverbal state, there was only the fear of nonexistence, because if I exist, then it could have happened that I would not have come into existence. So, there was the fear, the polarity of existence versus nonexistence, which set the karmic spiritual conundrum to be solved in this lifetime. It was already there. So, somebody asked something about karma. You can't come in at that level without having done a lot of prior spiritual work.

"I Am-Ness"

So, this is a state of exquisite bliss. It's rare, and half of those who go into it never come out of it. The sense "I Am," in God as "I Am" . . . It said, "Please define God." That's what brought all this on, folks. She shouldn't have asked that. "I Am-ness" I never understood. There was existence as existence. Then there was the corollary, the possibility of not existing. But there was never the thought of "I Am-ness." So, religious descriptions of God as I Am, or I Am That

Which I Am never had any reality for me. It still doesn't. Am-ness is a state of beingness, beingness. And the reality is beyond beingness or not-beingness. It's beyond existence versus nonexistence. It's certainly beyond beingness, so "I Am" is already redundant. It's already redundant. "Am-ness," like beingness, is an intransitive verb. That which is the ultimate reality requires no verbs, no adjectives; has no nouns; and doesn't need an intransitive verb of beingness, is-ness, was-ness, or anything-ness. It's beyond anything-ness, so I Am-ness, to me, is not exactly a valid statement; however, when we calibrate it, it comes out as 650.

"That Which I Am" as existence, anybody can reach through meditation. The letting go of identification with the physicality of the body itself; then letting go of the content of mind, becoming the witness of the content of mind; then becoming the awareness behind the experiencer of the witness of the content of the mind. You see, layer by layer you withdraw your identification from the particular, from the finite, from the definable, from the material. That Which I Am is the witness of All That Is, and the witness does not change depending on content.

How are you able to use language for the context of this reality when you feel you are energy, not form? How are you able to speak to people? It happens of its own. In the beginning it doesn't happen at all. There was no mention of it for 30 years. There's only a condition which prevented any participation in the world for a prolonged period of time. Then the body began to participate in the world again. I don't have time to check it out, but it's probably some karmic commitment or propensity to whether or not it continues. There's no necessity to continue, no necessity; but it goes about its business. It was a physician, so it went eventually back into practice. All human motivation disappeared. The mind is silent, and what the world calls "human" wasn't there anymore. Even the idea of serving others, helping the world, making a living—all those things that were meaningful, were void of—they didn't even exist. That which you are goes about that which it is, as an expression of the essence of that which it has evolved into over eons of time. So, this had the knowingness of the physician, psychiatrist, psychoanalyst practitioner. And it went back into practice, but when it did, the whole thing was totally different. It was the biggest practice in New York, and it specialized in severe illnesses—schizophrenia, primarily. The most hopeless of the hopeless came from all around the world. And this energy enabled the Self to recognize the Self within the entity that was all wrapped up and full of drugs, in a straitjacket on the floor. Instantly there's a recognition and an inner healing within the entity, and it's healed. Whether it recovers in the eyes of the world was something different. Sometimes it did. Sometimes it didn't. But the whole practice was transformed into a different way of being in the world. It went on of its own. Don't forget, it still goes on of its own. It goes on of its own right now. There was no discussion or mention of the inner state. No mention of the inner state. No mention of it until the writing of *Power vs. Force* in '95.

The calibrated scale of consciousness and kinesiology gave a bridge—how can the nonlinear be meaningful to the linear? Well, traditionally it really hasn't, because even religion doesn't understand the mystic. The enlightened person, once you go up the scale, you become what the world calls a "mystic." One's inner reality is what they're talking about, but there's no recognition by religion. Religion usually gets caught in conflict with the sage. Although it's the source of the reality of their own spiritual core of their own religion, the mystic is disavowed and very often considered a heretic. The way to get burned at the stake is to become a mystic in the Middle Ages. A bad time to get enlightened; 2000 is better. Because the reality as it is experienced is at variance with how it is described by God—I mean, by religion. I told you this morning that the negative views of God as an arbitrary punisher—that's insanity; that's the God of insanity. How insane can you be to not know the top of the box from the bottom of the box? Is God at the top? The source of the light? Or is it as religion says: He's at the bottom; the great punisher, waiting for you with whips and chains and tortures? Get away from it. I've been in hell, and no God would send anybody there. In fact, anybody who is evil wouldn't even send anybody there. It's beyond evil. It's beyond of any possibility of knowingness of what it could be. Never curse somebody to go there, folks. It's a really bad deal, because that which you condemn others to becomes your fate, you understand? You can't condemn somebody to hell without automatically precipitating some hellish conditions and experiences later in life.

I'll get to the raised hand in a second. I just wanted to finish this scale because somebody asked me about God, and that's really quite a discussion. "I Am-ness" never made sense to me. It still doesn't; it seems redundant. The word *I* is sufficient. "I" is complete and total, because the ultimate reality of God is the Source out of which consciousness and awareness arise. That which is Unmanifest then manifests as consciousness, which radiates forth as the light within which one knows the content of consciousness as form and mind and meaning and significance and all that it becomes within the linear domain as best expressed by Sir Isaac Newton.

The Death of the Ego

When Ramana Maharshi hit 700, he fell down at age 15—felt he was dying, which is correct. When the ego goes, it's death. The only death you can experience is the death of the ego. You can't experience death of the body, because you're out of body. The body is laying there. The death of the ego, the self, that is a whopper, and it takes all you've got to go through it. Ramana was not particularly religious. He was just going about daily life. One day he fell to the ground, felt he had died. He felt himself dying. When somebody feels themselves dying, you know that they have hit the end of the ego and that they're on the threshold of enlightenment, which is what he did. So, when he felt himself die, when I read he felt himself die, I knew this was the real thing, because that is exactly what happens. Then he went into a bliss state and sat there for weeks and didn't eat, didn't drink water; he was dehydrated and eaten up by bugs and stuff. It's comical, because it's just the way it is. So, anyway, the bugs were eating him, and he hadn't eaten anything or drunk anything, and he couldn't care less. He's just in this incredible state. Actually, he was in India where there were some spiritually sophisticated people that realized what had happened to him. They began to chase the bugs away, feed him, and get him to drink water, and all. And he didn't speak for two years. It's very funny, because in the meantime, a fake guru, of which the world abounds, started taking credit for his blissed-out state. He started signing up students right and left. Ramana, being in a mute state for two years, unable to speak or say anything, had nothing to do with it. Of course, he couldn't have cared less. This guy was making a living off him, so what's the difference? If you are a statue, let the birds use you how they will; you know it doesn't affect the fact that you're a statue! With coaxing and all, after about two years, Ramana began to learn how to speak.

So, finding the levels of consciousness gave a bridge to try to make the nonlinear comprehensible to the linear. As you go up the Scale of Consciousness, you see, you're going from that which is definable, measurable, scientifically verifiable, to that which is becoming more ineffable. As you cross over at 500, you've left the world of science. Science can't measure that—can't put it in a box; can't take its temperature; can't get its atomic weight; can't get its vibration on a spectrometer. It's left the world of science, the Newtonian paradigm of reality. So, 500, Love, is the real emergence of the nonlinear—the spiritual reality of the nonlinear, which is the Presence of God as Love. People say, "Where do you find God?" God is Love. God is everything—loving within yourself is already the Presence of God. How can you tell anybody who is interested in spiritual work and spiritual development has already within them the Presence of God that is pulling you like a magnet? It's not that you are pursuing God, but it's like the magnetism of the Self, That Which You Are, the Truth of That Which You Are is drawing you inevitably, inevitably like a moth to the flame. It can't be resisted.

So, here's Ramana Maharshi, practicing the mantra "I am all," or some simple-sounding thing. He really focused on it—and of course, the real critical thing that works in spiritual work, which we will get to in later lectures, is the fixity of focus. When you decide to really go for it, it means you cannot deviate from the edge of the knife for even one split second. If you're going to surrender every sensation, impulse, thought to God as it arises into the focus of consciousness, that has to be done with a fixity of purpose which is like a laser beam! Enormous intention, and you're not going to get off the edge of the knife for anything—sad, crying people on this side; wealth, happiness, radiation, seduction—nothing gets you off the edge of the knife. When you start that, you had better warn your friends, because the end is near. Devotion and dedication. The way of the heart, you see—to live on the edge of the knife requires an enormous devotion.

So, the way of mind, which I tend to talk about in public because I can't talk about the way of the heart—when you talk about the way of the heart, you very often can't start it, because the bliss state comes back, and you're whopped out of it, and that's the end of the lecture—people can come up and you can bless them, maybe.

You don't really have any say over it. There isn't any "you" to have a say. There isn't any "this" causing a "that." There isn't any center point of the ego/mind that is making decisions about what will be said. In ordinary consciousness, you think there's a "me" that's making a decision to say a "that." On top of that, you get purpose and intention, and it becomes very elaborate. I don't know how anybody manages. No. What happens is because of the nature, the quality of the Self within, with a capital S, the purusha—that core of the Self out of which the expression comes forth—happens of its own. The question arises from the audience. That affects the Self, which then speaks back through this person here, through this animal here. All right.

This experience here—now we're getting into the sense of "I," because as that state opened up, That Which I Am, That Which Is, is all that is, and the common nature through all of it is Divinity. That Which You Are, That Which Is; and it's the experience of reality as Allness. We mentioned the error of Void—is the ultimate reality Allness or Voidness? The ultimate reality is Allness. Allness. Out of the conundrum of the ultimate reality as Allness or

Nothingness arose a confirmation some 50 years later—or whatever it was—of Self as Allness. To realize that that which you call "I"—that which is the Self, that which is Divinity, and that which is All That Is—calibrates at 750. From 750 to 800, what happens is 30 years of silence, because the transformation is so stunning that you're struck dumb for 30 years. The mind doesn't think. To think in the presence of the Infinite Presence would be the ultimate absurdity. It's not even a possibility.

Out of that silence arose some kind of an awareness of this bridge and how it could be explained—how it could be explained. Yes, how it could be explained. This came about of its own—its understanding of the calibrated levels of consciousness as a way of making the nonlinear comprehensible to the linear. The human mind is used to scales, calibrations, temperatures; and therefore, the calibrated levels of consciousness seemed to make sense. We stumbled onto kinesiology as the ultimate tool, and that the field of consciousness is infallible because it's based on that which is, that which has reality, and therefore, it cannot be fooled. Therefore, the kinesiologic test is only a test of *yes*. It has no test of *no*. When the arm goes weak, it doesn't mean no; it merely means the absence of yes, because the infinite Reality is Allness and Existence and Truth. Its opposite has no existence. We used an example in previous lectures. There's only electricity going down a wire, or not electricity. There is no such thing as "nonelectricity" going down the wire. Electricity is either present or not present. You understand? Things are either present or not present. Absence is not a reality. You cannot take an armload of absence and bring me an armload of absence, any more than you can bring me an armload of nonexistence. There is no opposite to God.

The capacity to communicate this would be 800. That's a teacher of enlightenment. These are not great teachers, and the reason for that is, you can be the greatest piano virtuoso in the world, but that doesn't make you a good teacher of the piano. You can be Heifetz but be a very bad violin teacher. To be the virtuoso is one thing; to be able to convey it to others and to teach it to others is something else. It's like a separate, karmic kind of commitment, I would say. Most likely, a commitment: "We have permission to ask this, resist." (True.) "That was a prior karmic commitment, resist." (True.)

Now, at 840, what occurred in this lifetime at age three or four was the confrontation, the confrontation with the ultimate reality as existence or nonexistence. Were nonexistence a possibility, whence would it arise? Existence, you see, because the Unmanifest becomes manifest . . . As it becomes manifest, the God as the Godhead—you might say the Godhead is the Unmanifest out of which Divinity arises, and the nature of Divinity is creation. And henceforth, everything that evolves out of creation itself has the capacity for creation, so all is in the process of being created as well as being creator, you might say.

The Newtonian Paradigm of Causality

Things are not arising in the world out of causality. They are arising out of creation. Everything . . . what we call "thing"—what the mind calls "event" is not sequential. It's only sequential from the viewpoint of the observer. Because you perceive things sequentially, you think that one thing is causing another. If we have these balls A, B, C, D, the world assumes that you hit A with a cue stick and that hits B and that causes C and that causes D. That's the Newtonian paradigm of causality. Actually, the way it comes about is, that which causes A is simultaneously the cause of B, is exactly and simultaneously the same as the cause of C, and is simultaneously the cause of D. It takes the totality of God to account for the existence of everything at any moment, anywhere in time. Otherwise, God would have merely set the billiard ball rolling, disappeared off into heaven. That's the trouble with religion; God is transcendent. That's where the mystic gets himself burned at the stake. He says, "No, God is immanent." That which is the Source of life itself, within oneself—the source of existence and reality, the source of the awareness of your existence is the Presence of God as within, as Self as the ultimate reality. And that is the truth of the enlightened sage, who says that God is not only transcendent, but immanent. He doesn't say that. The sage knows that which is immanent is also transcendent—they are not opposites; they're only two different ways of looking at it. That which is transcendent obviously would have to be immanent, and that which is immanent would obviously, by definition, also have to be transcendent. To say that God is either transcendent or immanent—the Presence of God is realized as immanent, then we say the person is enlightened, sage, or whatever you want to call it.

The Avatar, then, beyond Self and Existence—the Avatar is at 985. That power is sufficient to influence mankind throughout all of time. What's the difference between 985 and 1000? I only came upon it recently. I was explaining in a lecture or two, writing, or something, the obvious nature of reality as it appears and then realized that the Buddha differed. We calibrated the Buddha's law of endless causation. So, what I just said already differed from what the Buddha thought: the endless causation, that the cause of one thing is an endless series of causes—but to see a cause, you would have to have something that is caused, and to see something that is caused is already within the world of form. To see that everything is coming out of the spontaneity of creation, out of the essence of that which it is, calibrates at 1000. The law of infinite causation, dependent causation calibrates at 985. We just discovered that this week, or something.

So, the great enlightened beings of all time, who had not only the capacity of the knowingness but the capacity to express it in society in a way that was sufficiently meaningful that it recontextualized all of society for a thousand years—so, that's "I" as the ultimate reality, the subject of the book I'm finishing. That that which you experience as self, that you say, "When I say, 'I'"—how can you experience your own existence? You experience that which I am as "I," the pronoun *I*. It's very interesting that the pronoun *I* is capitalized just as the *G* is in "God." The only pronoun that is capitalized is *I*. You would think, out of humility, mankind would have made himself a small *i* and God the big *I*, but he didn't. Why is *I* the same as *God*? *I* is capitalized, and so is *God*. Is that grandiosity, megalomania, insanity, what? Huh? No. It's because the truth is that the personal "I" can only be known by virtue of the Infinite "I" which underlies it. Because of the universality and the infinite knowingness of the "I" of the Self, the Presence of God within, conveys to you the capacity to be aware of your own existence as the small "i." So, the small "i" knows that it is by virtue of the Infinite "I" which is the source of its consciousness, awareness, and existence. To know Self as "I." So, the ultimate statement, "Please define God," then is, God is the Infinite "I" within. And without. The Infinite "I" of all that exists. Beyond all dimensions, beyond all planes, beyond all universes, beyond all divisions.

Therefore, you do not want to bring down the level "I" by saying "Am-ness." Because "I" as the Infinite Reality is 1000. And "I" as "Am-ness" is already a considerable condensation, because now you've put the condition of "beingness" and "Is-ness" upon it. "Beingness" and "Is-ness" means to come into manifestation, but the Infinite "I," That Which You Really Are, is the Unmanifest. The Infinite "I" is the Unmanifest. To say, "I Am" means that you are now manifest; it limits the realization of that which you are. At this moment, one experiences oneself as manifest, but that doesn't mean it is the Ultimate Reality any more than you are your body or you are your mind.

CHAPTER 3

THE ENLIGHTENED AND DIVINE STATES

The "I," the Self, the God of all universes, of which there are an infinite number, is 1250. To go from around 700 or so, which doesn't happen very often, on upward is not a pleasant experience. It's not like the high 500s. It is not exquisite kundalini energy coming up through you and pouring out through yourself exquisitely. What happens now—or what happened here and happened with the Buddha—was, the nervous system is overly taxed and goes into exquisite pain. It's like a burning sensation, like the nerves have become barbed wire, red-hot barbed wire. It's a horrible sensation. It's throughout your whole aura. You can't escape it, no matter what. And this means that there's some awareness "out." This signifies that there's something holding up the progression. Maybe that only happens if you're karmically destined to progress. So, if you have the misfortune of this karmically destined to progress, this consciousness keeps going, and it's not satisfied with 700, but it should be. It's absolute totality, infinite bliss—the knowingness of the Oneness of the Divine Presence, but something out of someplace can force it to grow, and it goes beyond that. Then there are these horrible experiences which go on for years. You can be driving along perfectly fine, and suddenly a thought goes through the air somewhere and this extreme discomfort starts. You find out what the error is, and you correct the error, usually in the form of a prayer, and then it disappears. So, this goes on for quite a painful period of time.

At the time of which the mind disappeared, it was obliterated by an infinite Presence of crystal clarity and exquisite beauty, exquisite gentleness, and profound power beyond all imagination. All conceptions of power compared to the power of the Presence is infinitesimal. So, the mind is, like, whatever is left of the mind, is, like, obliterated. And for fun, some 30 years later, when I learned kinesiology, I asked . . . "That was the thought of an archangel, resist." (True.) That will give you some idea of power. In the pits of hell, the atheist says, "If there is a God, I ask him to help me." Then infinite silence; then suddenly this infinite Presence—absolute silence, and it was like you grabbed onto a 50,000-volt—the power was so infinite. "So, the response to the prayer was a thought, was a thought by that archangel; correct, karmically thought." (True.)

It was like an archangel was cruising by and he hears this screech from the pits of hell, and he gives it a thought—instantly, that which you were is totally obliterated for all time, and the radiance shines forth, and there you are, barely able to see in the light. It just gave you a passing thought. This is as good a way to describe it as anything, how it comes about.

All's an evolution of consciousness, and we call that evolution "karmic." The word *karma* here does not mean "reincarnation." Karma means that consciousness evolves, and each thing becomes an expression of its essence, and we call that "karma." You can't be a human being here, sitting in a body without already a karmic inheritance that allows you to do so, so there's no point to worry about karma—because that which you are *is* your karma. The ego is your karma. There's no necessity to look for where it arose from, any more than it's not too interesting how you broke an ankle. The problem is how to fix it, you know what I mean? As a physician, I don't care how you broke it—fell down a case of stairs, you were having a battle with your wife—that's all immaterial. You want to fix what the condition is now, because the condition *now* is the inheritance of the past. It was the walking down the steps, the slipping on the banana peel, the argument with the spouse, the not paying attention. So, however it arose karmically . . . as spiritual students, our presentation is how we experience ourselves in the present moment as compared to how we would like to become in due time.

So, we said the archangel is 50,000 and up. 50,000 and up; 50,000 for jacks, for openers. And the Supreme and Ultimate Realization, of course, is God as Unmanifest as well as Manifest. Because that which is manifest is both manifest and beyond both. The Ultimate Reality is beyond either Manifest or Unmanifest, all of which are definitions of mind, and when mind stops, they're meaningless.

Mantras

What's the value of a mantra? It depends . . . calibrating levels of energy is useful. Let's take the mantra *Ohm*. "The mantra *Ohm* calibrates over 600." (True.) "700." (True.) "720." (True.) "740." (True.) "750." (True.) "The mantra *Ohm* is in the 700s—resist." (True.)

Now let's try *Aum*. "The mantra *Aum*—A-U-M—is over 600." (Not true.) "It is over 300. Aum, 300." (True.) "It's over 310." (Not true.) Whether you go "Ohm" or "Aum" makes quite a bit of difference! If you go "Aum," you are going to take a long time to get enlightened, right?

So, one reason for the lectures is that the comprehension speaking to you now is capable of explaining things that have been misunderstood. The reason for writing the books is to clarify things that are obvious—Obvious with a capital O, but not obvious with a small o. So, the purpose of these 12 lectures is to fortify that which is known, in such a way that it is not misinterpreted later. To fortify it with such a bulwark of explanation, demonstration, and clarification that it can't be misunderstood. The ultimate mantra is either "Ohm" or "Aum," right?

So, the purpose is, first of all, to provide sufficient information that it would be sufficient to take one the whole way. To share the subjective reality of it, and also to provide a tool by which the person, like a compass, can find their own way through the woods. And to also warn of the pitfalls, where many fall off. Seduction by that which sounds exotic, especially if it comes from some other realm. Everything from some other realm is called "spiritual." There are many realms, and many of them are not where you want to go; nor do you want to follow their advice. Yet it is commonly done because it comes from Master Gump-Gump on the other side. So, you go to this school, and Baba Buchi is talking to me. He says, "You should sell your livestock and move to Cincinnati and go out in the field and wait for the UFOs to come and greet you." "Thank you, Baba."

No, if you're going to do any channeling trances, messages from the other side, you'd better calibrate them. Always calibrate the entity on the other side. Because there are good people, because there are different realms. There's higher astral and lower astral. The highest higher astrals are called "celestial." There are multiple heavens. There are multiple purgatories. There are multiple hells. And there are entities in various regions that would like to have influence in the human domain that hate the human domain because the human domain contains the capacity to realize God, and the lower-astral domain are those who have refused God, cursed God, or blasphemed God, as we demonstrated before with kinesiology. And which, as Jesus Christ said, cannot be forgiven. In other words, the belief in an Avatar as one's savior is necessary up to level 600. And the savior can act in your behalf. Lotus Land Buddhism teaches that. Christianity teaches that. The Buddha of Infinite Compassion can speak for you and you go to Lotus Land, which is heaven. The Buddha becomes your intercessor. So, you earn by devotion the right of an intercessor to speak in your behalf, because you of your own level of consciousness are not able to transcend all the domains. So, the Christ speaks for you, the Buddha speaks for you, other saviors speak for you. And in that energy field, all can be forgiven. But it says some things cannot be forgiven, and it is well to pay attention, because that is a fact. It cannot be wiped off your slate by a great spiritual Master. If it cannot be wiped off your slate by a great spiritual Master, then it is undone by your living it out, experiencing it out. And the time in hell is beyond time. Don't forget that the lower levels of hell are just like the higher levels. They're beyond the form of time.

And the lower levels of hell are beyond description. The agony is infinite, and it's forever. Because it's forever, the horror of what has happened to you dawns on you. Therefore, to undo it, karmically one experiences that to which they have cursed somebody else. And now you experience the hell that you cursed them to, et cetera.

Celestial Realms and Teachers

There are various realms—heavenly realms; the higher astral are commonly called "celestial." In the experiences I've described to you today, there was never any other entity there. On the way to hell, I passed no devils. Dante was correct. Dante's description of hell is literally correct, exactly the way it is. The upper levels are torture and torment and agony and suffering and dismemberment, et cetera. But those are just jacks for openers. Then you get to the real hell. All that stops, and a nameless dread, which goes on for eons, prevails. In the higher realms, there are celestial beings, and many of them have been described in spiritual literature—the Great White Brotherhood, the visions of the saints. These are, to me, the higher celestial realms in which form still persists. The idea of an "other" is not conceivable when form disappears as a reality; there is no *this* and an "other" *that*. So, it's not within this experience of higher beings, guides, and spiritual divine figures that come to you. They must be in the higher celestial. "What this is asking about is the higher celestial." (True.) All right. So, there are celestial realms still within form—you might say "lower heavens" where form persists—and divine figures. And frankly that is good enough. I'll take lower heavens anytime. It is a wonderful place.

Form can then persist as devils. People experience the presence of demonic figures, hellish figures in the lower-astral domains; and saintly figures and spiritual guides and angels in the higher— in the others. I pretty much restrict myself to that which has been experienced as a reality; other things, I've only heard about. So, I differentiate that which I have heard about and that which I know. I've never had to meet celestial beings.

In calibrating, there's a current book I am working on called *All Stands Revealed*. Chief Detroit calibrates at 700. He has a very famous quotation that persists to this day. The structure of the United States government is very much just nothing but the way it was in the Iroquois Nation. Anyway, Chief Detroit calibrates at 700, and the Native American Great White Spirit calibrates as a very high understanding of God, because it's God as present both transcendent and immanent—in other words, the divinity of all living things. The Native American sees the divinity of all that exists, which is put down in theology as "pantheism." Once you label a thing, you lose what it is. To see that the deer is divine is to be aware of the ultimate reality, that the Great White Spirit expresses itself as all of life; as all of life. The Native American was quite enlightened spiritually.

You can't really compare teachers. Each teacher is what it is. If you calibrate the teaching of a teacher or the book by the teacher, you will end up with a different calibration level. There are great teachers that are in the 500s. Once in a while, you will hit one as high as 700. The Bhagavad Gita calibrates about 1000: the teachings of Krishna. Each teacher is teaching from a different level.

The reason I talk about levels of consciousness is to know what level is being spoken of. If you read Ramana Maharshi and he tells you, "Don't bother to save the world, because the world you see doesn't even exist," that's about 740. But that's not the reality of the reader. We say, "What about the starving children? What about the cat that just got run over and has a broken leg?" Is that meaningful, or what? So, a teacher may be useful to you within a certain range. Teachers come up at various parts of your lifetime because of your karmic momentum, the place that you're at. So, what is meaningful to you at one level may not be meaningful to you at another. It's like comparing apples and oranges.

Certain approaches will appeal to you, and others will not. Some approaches will appeal to you at certain times in your life and not at other times. *The Transmission of Mind*—even the title, people say, "Huh?" Huang Po, *The Transmission of Mind*. That's about, what, 740? "Huang Po, *Transmission of No Mind*, is over 700." (True.) "720." (True.) "730." (True.) "740." (True.) "750." (True.) "760." (Not true.) About 750.

What we're talking about and we're leading to in these lectures—there's a lecture on Advaita, the way to God—it said, "through Mind"—but its reality is the way to God through "No Mind." The only way to get to No Mind is through Mind, and so therefore, we'll get to No Mind through Mind by approaching it from No Mind. Okay. Now, that is meaningful to me.

Levels of Consciousness of Institutions and Companies

This asks the specific calibrations of a number of people and government institutions. We calibrated the FBI and the CIA, and the Alcohol, Tobacco and Firearms—ATF. At the time, the ATF, CIA, and FBI all made you go weak. And I think it's on that tape we did in '95. The third level from the top in the CIA had a mole. And there was a serious mole at a high level in the FBI. They have since hit the news. Generally, government agencies calibrate about 202. It seems to me they are integrous because the law insists that they be that way—but they're not happy about it! Nor do you get much helpfulness or cheerfulness about it. It's like you are at the Motor Vehicle Bureau: "You forgot to sign on line six. You've got to go back at the end of the line." Not just, you know, "Why not sign here and hand it to me." No. "You've got to go back to the end of the line." I mean, where's the heart? That is 200. "Listen, that's my job. I know my job, I have my job and I do my job." That's 200; I know my job and I do my job. And you cannot fire them because they're doing their job. But you're not happy to be with them, and they don't seem too happy with who they are or what their job is. So, it's perfunctory; 200 is perfunctory. It's integrous. If it says you've got to be there from eight to five, by God, they're there from eight to five. And if it says it's your job to run this computer and run these lists through here, that's what they do. It's dependable in that it complies with the requirements of the job description, but it does not offer much beyond that. Cheerfulness is something else.

I always say the application of the levels of consciousness to business are quite profound. A few people who've been here and a few people we work with are endeavoring to take spiritual teaching into the commerce and industry business. As long as you don't label it spiritual, religious, or God, you get away with it. You can take it in the back door by calling it "integrity that builds customer confidence which shows up in the bottom line." And it does.

In *Power vs. Force,* I used Walmart as an example because I had corresponded with Sam Walton and I recognized the integrity. Sam's ideal was integrity: integrous products by integrous people in integrous surroundings, and his idea of treating employees was considerate, and et cetera. He seemed to have heart. "Walmart at the time of Sam Walton is over 350." (True.) "380." (True.) "390." (Not true.) "Walmart at the time of Sam Walton was 385." (True.) "390." (Not true.) 385—remember what 385 is on our list? It is up there. It beats 200. I'd rather walk into Sam Walton's business than the nearest Motor Vehicle Bureau.

Sam took his business up to Harmonious, Hopeful, Satisfactory; you can trust in him—"made in America"—optimistic, forgiveness—we don't ask any questions; bring it back and we'll give you a refund or a replacement. "Walmart at this time is below 385, resist." (True.) "It is about 325." (True.) "330." (Not true.)

This last week's issue of *Fortune* magazine had a big article on Walmart, and it said that Walmart isn't exactly as great as it was at the time of Sam. I thought they were nitpicking a little bit, but Walmart has become a giant colossus. It's hard to keep that folksy, rural atmosphere when you're the biggest retailer in the world. How do you keep it folksy when you have got—one million employees? Can you believe a company that has one million employees, and a major outlet in every major city in America, and now crossing the world in Asia, and all? Sam built what has become the largest, most successful retailing experience in human history. And he did it from the integrity of 385. Anybody who questions whether or not spiritual values have any serious application to a business, they only have to look at Walmart.

It's funny—a writer from the *Wall Street Journal* called us up a month or two ago, writing an article on this subject, wanting my views on "the value of spiritual principles in the corporate world." I referred him to Magali's article. So, to answer the question, "Do spiritual values have any practical application in the everyday world?" Well, we just tell them to look at Walmart and see for yourself. Would you rather go to Walmart, or would you rather go to renew your license at the nearest Motor Vehicle Bureau?

The government agencies, if you calibrate them all, it's pretty disappointing. The FAA, for instance, extremely low. If you calibrate what is the level of integrity of the agency as an agency, you will usually get around 200. Then we discovered, but "what is the calibrated level of their everyday functioning in the world"—then you get a disappointment. Although the FAA may calibrate as an agency in its formal structure, bureaucracy at 200, what does it operate at? "There's a disparity, resist." (True.) "The disparity is over 50 points, resist." (True.) Oh my God. "We have permission to ask the FAA, resist." (True.) "The FAA as a bureaucratic agency calibrates over 200, resist." (Not true.) Oh, it doesn't. "It calibrates over 198." (True.) Oh my God, it's gotten worse. Last time we did this, I think it was 200. "It's over 198." (True.) "199." (Not true.)

It's not quite integrous, even at the bureaucratic level. Let's get what it is at the operational level. "The FAA operationally is over 140." (Not true.) All right, let's say, the structure is integrous, but the way it is instituted is totally nonintegrous. And you can tell by the everyday news the way the FAA functions. Here's the people you're trusting your life to when you're getting on a plane.

A lot can be learned, and once you see the panorama, it's like you've got the map of human civilization. And when you calibrate Henry VIII, Julius Caesar, Franklin Delano Roosevelt, Churchill . . . Churchill calibrated at 510; FDR calibrated at 499. Most of the presidents of the United States calibrate in the 450s. You can ask: What is the requirement of this office? The requirement to be an effective president of the United States is about 450. Happily, almost all of our presidents have been 450 or over, or 460. If you ask, "What does it take to run a giant world church?" The pope, for instance—the ideal for a religious leader to run a world organization such as the Catholic Church is around 570. If you go to 600, you're going to bliss out. They're not going to go to church—they're not going to pay attention to you. You have to have a lot of organizational ability, a lot of political moxie, a lot of knowingness; you've got to be able to deal with all the heads of state; you have to do this in the context of a religious history that goes back thousands of years and is under fire, et cetera; and a complex political state. So, you need around 570—almost saintly. And if you watch Pope John Paul II as he tries to make peace with the various factions around the world, you get a sense of presence. The Dalai Lama serves the same function—a world function as the leader of a world church and all that it represents. The Dalai Lama is also around 570.

Mother Teresa is about 700. Bush is around 460 or so. He's a Yale graduate, a very smart man. You have to deal in the world of form, politics, power, bureaucracy, fundraising, charm, and verbal capacity. You know he is integrous on the level that he represents. You may or may not agree with his level, but he does come out of an old-fashioned, right-or-wrong, Christian-oriented, good ol' Texas boy. He has integrity on a moral level. The president of a university has a different requirement. So, you can't say that one level is better than another; you have to say, "Better for what?" Otherwise we are comparing apples and oranges.

The highest calibrated unit that we got in World War II was the Tuskegee Air Force. The Tuskegee Air Force had the most perfect record, the greatest number of kills, the smallest number of losses. These were all high-level people in which intention was extremely powerful. And they set up one of the greatest records in World War II. So, you learn a great deal by studying history, calibrating the levels of the various events. You can calibrate the level of the events. You can, with kinesiology, find out exactly what happened. Was the U.S. informed before Pearl Harbor or not? Who was informed? What did they do with it, and why? I don't like to do a lot of these things in public. But what goes on behind the scenes is accessible because anything that's registered in the field of consciousness is available to kinesiology. When you ask a question with kinesiology, we ask permission. Sometimes you'll get a no. Sometimes you'll get a flat no. Sometimes you'll get a—if you try to find out the *why* of the no, you may or may not find out the why of no. Usually you'll find out the why of the no. Sometimes you won't even get the why of the no.

We've said that the time of death is karmically set. Can you find out the time of your own death? You'll always get the answer no. It would probably have a deleterious effect, wouldn't it? The churches would be loaded, though, if everybody knew!

Nevertheless, we can check out the great gurus of history. As I have said, a lot of the great gurus are not, as living beings, what they were at the highest of their writings, because, you might say, that which is in contrast to that which you become. As you go up in levels of consciousness, you begin to pull to yourself that which challenges it. There are certain levels at which rather specific things come at you. And I think a spiritual teacher should inform you of the downside. Unconditional Love seems to trigger a state of joy. It seems to bring up its opposite choice. In this particular experience, that which brought it up was quite surprising. It comes up suddenly out of nowhere. It can come up through a person.

This person I was speaking to was a spiritual teacher, well-known—and well-known locally, in fact—who had described an excellent spiritual technique. All of a sudden, this spiritual teacher wanted me to be director of this organization nationwide. I said, "Wow, we can give it to all the monks and all the monasteries, and just think of all the people struggling with sin—and sin is just an attachment." If you know how to release the attachment, sin disappears. Sin is just a pejorative epithet with which we describe certain behaviors, but the behaviors are just attachments. So, I wanted to give it to the world, and I thought, *Oh, wow. Give the world a way to free yourself from guilt and sin and all this crap.* At this point the teacher suddenly went into a rage. The teacher's personality disappeared, and it was like an entity from hell. It was a horrible energy. And he suddenly began to speak in another voice and said, "Jesus and Buddha are just astrals! You should never give away spiritual truth. A thing is only as good as what you pay for it. The higher the truth, the more the charge." He began to describe certain industrialists as having done more for mankind than Jesus Christ and Buddha, because they were just astrals. And then the conversation got even worse.

Power for Its Own Sake

The temptation in that case was Luciferic: pain, suffering, war, rape, pillage, drugs, devastation, street gangs. Power for its own sake. The manifestation of power is financial gain. And what happens on that level of consciousness was . . . a knowingness came to me, a knowingness. This was beyond . . . this was the experimentation with going into the Void. That which is the Void, in this lifetime was triggered again, and the way you get to the Void of nothingness is by releasing the attributes of God. Seeing love is an attachment, beauty, the Grace of God; attachments are holding you back from the Ultimate Truth. The Luciferic persuasion can sound quite convincing. It came as a knowingness. There was nobody there, but the knowingness came as an expression: "Now that you know you're beyond personal karma . . ."—because at that point, one is beyond form; it was a quite enlightened state. Let's see what level that temptation came at. "That temptation came at over 600." (True.) "650." (True.) "700." (True.) "720." (Not true.) About 720. The knowingness was, "Now that you know you're beyond personal karma, because you're not answerable to any arbitrary God, because no such God exists, and you've already transcended identification with all of form and the human ego; therefore, own infinite power as your own." Well, it came across as a very convincing understanding. It obviously had been presented to many others in the past. This was a rather arid—it was almost like compared to a high mountain pass. No one there. No one had hardly ever been there. I could see who had been there and what answer they had given. The appeal was infinite power—power over others, power for its own sake, power for its own sake.

Of course, what was wrong with it was, it was completely devoid of love; no love.

Just power—to own power for its own sake is apparently a temptation. So, the spiritual student who's not prepared for it goes into a very high state and begins to pull up its . . . I am going to call it its "contrary" choice. So, to choose power for its own sake, then, is the temptation of the Luciferic when you get to a very high level. The Luciferic is the temptation of power for its own sake, usually expressed in our domain as wealth. So, a company like Enron is the expression of the Luciferic. The satanic would be Adolph Hitler. The Luciferic is money and wealth and power and position for its own sake.

The satanic would use that to cause suffering to others, so Nazi Germany, the Japanese in Nanking exhibit satanic energy. So, the temptation can come up and you are unprepared for it. And the ingenuity with which it can be presented, I am underplaying. It can be extremely ingenious. It's probably been developed for thousands of years by various entities who rule other domains, and what they're really inviting you to is to join their domain and become one of them, just as the Mafia invites you to become a "made" guy by executing this guy in front of witnesses. They invite you to join and become a part of the satanic lower-astral realm.

So, those things apparently happen to various people at various times. It can happen to people within the secular domain as well as in the spiritual domain. In calibrating the levels of consciousness of people throughout time, we've said: Napoleon started out quite high, then fell to the megalomania. So, the other temptation is that of vanity. If we said that the top of the levels of consciousness is God, then the bottom is the ego. The bottom is the ego and the glorification of the ego as God. The "i," the small "i,"—to glorify the small "i," to worship the small "i" is to become the egomaniac. So, when Milosevic feels not the slightest contrition, feels it's his perfect right to destroy millions of people mainly because they disagree with him or represent something he does not like, this is the expression of megalomania. So, the ego, the unbridled ego, then, when it is glorified becomes the opposite of God, which entitles the person to go to the lower-astral domains. So, a person is there by choice by denying the reality of God and declaring that the ego is God. That makes the "i," the small "i" the center of the ego as God, instead of divinity as God. That's how one gets to the bottom instead of the top.

The difficulty with religions has been their confusion with the top and the bottom. As I have said before, the Old Testament is the source of that. If you check out the Old Testament with kinesiology, all the books of the Old Testament make you go weak, with the exception of three: Proverbs, Psalms, and Genesis. All the rest make you go extremely weak. In the New Testament, of course, Revelation calibrates at 70. Its author is John. Let's see what the source of Revelation is: "The source of Revelation is a fellow named John, resist." (True.) "He calibrates at 70, resist. (True.) "What he had was a hallucination and vision of the lower-astral domain, resist." (True.)

Reality within the Astral Domain

So, all these predictors, these revelations of horrors such as California falling off into the ocean, the end times, is all true, but it's only true within the astral domain. So, one thing a spiritual student has to be clear is, what applies to the astral domain applies to the astral domain, in which there's a replica of this world as we know it—but it has a different karma. It is ruled by different entities and energies. So, what is predicted for the astral domain is not what is predicted for this earth. There are a number of teachers around Sedona who had the same vision. Everybody got ready for the end times, dug underground homes, et cetera, sat around waiting for the end times. California did not fall off in the ocean; the end times did not occur. To not realize which domain you're speaking of—to be clear, if confused you can check with kinesiology: "The end times is describing a different domain, resist." (True.) It is a different domain. If you experience that domain, you experience it as reality. It is not like imagination. It is when you are in that domain, then you experience the experience of that domain as a reality. A person who slips because of brain chemistry over into that reality experiences that as though it is actually happening. And the reason you can't get them out of saying that they experienced it as really happening is because they *did* experience it as really happening. A dream is real when you're in the dream. A nightmare is an experiential reality. In the middle of the nightmare, you are experiencing that nightmare as a reality. That that nightmare is not the same as the waking domain of reality is, of course, the differentiation between the two.

So, a lot of the spiritual errors that have arisen, religious errors, have arisen because of lack of capacity to know one domain from another. Lower-astral domains, just like the higher are ruled by entities. Each of them has names. The gods of the celestial regions have names, and so do the gods of the lower astral-regions.

Strict and narrow is the pathway. The Buddha was correct. He also described similar temptations, as did Jesus Christ. The Luciferic came to him directly the same way. Undoubtedly the same entity, the same energy. Was that the same energy? "It's an entity, resist." (Not true.) It's not an entity, no. It's a knowingness of a certain energy field, and it comes into your consciousness that way.

What I am trying to convey is from experience as well as available literature. The spiritual student is often naive; wanders off in the desert with a pint of water and a pair of sandals. It takes more than a pint of water and a pair of sandals to reach enlightenment. It's a strict and narrow pathway. It's rigorous; it's demanding; it's beset with pitfalls. That which is in the lower astral, its greatest pleasure is to pull people off the straight and narrow. The fact that you are on the straight and narrow is what makes you a nice prize, a nice plump one to pull off with one temptation or another. That is the source of glee of the demonic—that they have seduced an innocent one. To kill the innocent is the way you rise in the lower astral. It's by killing innocent babies that you really get to be somebody. Take a bayonet and bayonet the child—the infant in the mother's arms—gets you really up in the hierarchy. It gets you higher than the Mafia. The Mafia only kills bad guys. You have got to be cold, heartless, cruel—the ultimate of the opposite of goodness.

All these various realms have their own hierarchies. They're complex. They have their own literature. There are a lot of well-known books in the spiritual bookstore, which all of you know. You have all run into them. Let's ask about one: "*The Urantia Book* calibrates over 200, resist." (Not true.) *The Urantia Book* is well-known. It's a channeling from some other domain. In the Urantia hierarchy of beings and teachers is even Jesus Christ. So, before you get enamored of any spiritual teaching, calibrate the energy field of the teaching. And the other thing you're going to ask is whether it's "suitable for me." It may be a very high teaching, and I say, "Is that suitable for me?" And it says no. Why? Because at this level, I would misinterpret it. It would be injurious. So, the willingness to surrender to God means to—let's say, operationally, if you get a no from a kinesiologic question—to question "Why?" come up with an answer and then the willingness to comply with it.

All pathways are pathways through the heart because all pathways are the willingness to surrender the ego's delusion that it is capable of knowing reality. The ego is not capable of knowing reality. By definition, the ego *can't* know reality—Reality with a capital *R*. By definition, it's a telescope that doesn't go that far, you know what I mean? It's a 12x telescope, and you're trying to see into the next galaxy. You can't see into the next galaxy with a 12x, you know what I mean?

Spiritual Disillusionment

In this section, we've covered a lot of stuff—enough to offend at least a half dozen people! If we calibrate your favorite spiritual teacher and found out he's only 42, well . . . somebody's got to tell you. Spiritual disillusionment is very, very painful. To become enamored of a certain teacher and then later discover that teacher is not integrous is horrible. These people, I've seen some in the office. Some I've known in the spiritual community. It's worse than a marital infidelity. It's worse than the boss telling lies behind your back. It's like the ultimate double-crossing. It's like the devil. There are all kinds of gurus that calibrate below 200. And I've traveled a little bit around the spiritual circuit myself. You see pictures of this guru there, and the incense is going, and hearts and flowers and fruit, and the guy calibrates 120—you know what I'm saying? It takes more than sandals, incense and robes, and shaved head and sitting on tiger skin to make a guru.

The Buddha was a teacher about "right livelihood," one of the Eightfold Pathway. It means to be integrous in one's endeavors within the world by which you make a living. He recommended that you not be a butcher and things like that; that the accumulated negative karma of constantly killing life in return for money would undo a great deal of spiritual merit. Buddhism and Far Eastern language tend to talk of spiritual merit. So, integrity has to do with intention. We've said spiritual level has to do with intention. When you do spiritual work, you're really doing it from the center of your spiritual will. You want to get away from thinking there's a personal "I" doing that. There's no personal "I" there. Consciousness is impersonal. You make a decision from your spiritual will. It's your spiritual will because your spiritual will has infinite power. Your spiritual will is unstoppable. Spiritual will allows you to get burned at the stake and not flinch an inch from what you believe in. That takes spiritual will. The ego doesn't have that kind of strength. The mind doesn't have that kind of strength. Spiritual will, though, is extremely powerful. That is why the Buddha said, "Once you've heard of enlightenment, the end is certain." Once you've even heard of enlightenment, the end is certain. Because once the spiritual will hears that enlightenment is possible, it clicks onto it and now it begins to reorganize the intention of all the intricacies of the ego. And somehow, you just find yourself in the right place and moving in a certain direction. That's a result of spiritual will.

So, integrity, then, is a decision. The reason I used Sam Walton as an example was because he seemed to represent in a widely experiential way the value of integrity in business. Because of that integrity which radiates out, the consumer has confidence. That if it's broken and you take it back, they'll give you another one. Of course, experientially I have done that, and by God, they do give you another one. If they cannot give you another one, they fix it. So, at least, there's the intention of integrity. Integrity is extremely important, I think, in the spiritual community. In government it would be profoundly unworkable. How are you going to get reelected if you're going to be integrous, you know what I mean? You would have to be honest, and how would you get elected? Some variance with integrity is necessary on certain levels.

Illumination and Enlightenment

What is the difference between illumination and enlightenment? Generally, "illuminated" refers to 600 and over. It's denoted in art, usually, as a halo. If you calibrate the energy level of the halo, that which it signifies is 1000: sainthood or above. The general public would say that anybody into the high 500s is already illuminated. We think of the saintly person as reflecting the light of Divinity by their patience and all the classic virtues: patience and tolerance and truthfulness and integrity. "Illumination is over 550." (True.) "580." (True.) "590." (True.) "599." (True.) "600." (True.) "601." (Not true.)

600 is the level of illumination. It's because the Presence of the Self is felt like a light that it's seen as the light of consciousness. You're conscious of that which, in ordinary life, you take for granted and never realize what it is. You never look at it. Just like in this room, you're aware of the contents of the room, but you're not aware of the space in the room. I mean, your focus is not on the space here. Your focus is on the content. Enlightenment becomes that you're aware of the field; you're aware of the field itself out of which the content becomes meaningful. It's because of the non-form of the field that the world of form makes any sense. It's by virtue of that which is nonlinear that anything linear can be discerned. If space wasn't full of nothingness, you couldn't see "somethingness" in it.

Now, consciousness is the quality that would allow the awareness of beingness. The fact that you realize, you know that you are. Let's ask about the cat: "Kitty knows that he *is*—resist." (True.) You might say that's primordial, right? Primordial. It is by virtue of consciousness that Kitty is aware that he is. "Kitty has consciousness." (True.) "Which comes out of existence." (True.) "Kitty has knowingness of existence." (True.) "Kitty has capacity to identify it, resist." (Not true.) It can't identify it but knows that it is. When you look into any animal's eyes, it's instantly obvious that it knows that it is. It knows that it is. It's aware of existence.

You see, existence is a statement. Beingness—*being* is an intransitive verb. "Is-ness," "beingness," "havingness," "is-ness" are all verbs. In a verb, there has to be a "this" and a "that." When you add "beingness" or "am-ness," you're saying that there is "something" that has that quality. That's why "am-ness" has not described to me what the Ultimate Reality is. "Am-ness" implies that there is "something" that *has* that quality of "beingness." That's what an intransitive verb means. That implies a duality which is not my own experience of reality, which is nonduality. The radical truth is, there is no "this" experiencing a "that," such as a quality of "beingness" or "is-ness." That awareness is illuminated by virtue of consciousness itself. So, that statement came out of consciousness about beingness.

Questions from the Audience

Q: *"You indicated that at 600 and above, the higher levels of consciousness, that the body would become incapacitated."*

It's not that the body is incapacitated; it's more that one's indifferent to it. The state is so complete and perfect—then there is no wantingness. You see, to move something, you have to have a wantingness. All wantingness disappears.

I think many of the basic physiologic functions do stop. Breathing will even stop. And only if somebody entreats you, do you breathe again. I had no interest in breathing again. But somebody loved me a great deal. I could see that he believed that I would be dead if I didn't breathe. Because of his belief that I would be dead, I breathed.

Q: *"Did Jesus and Krishna and Buddha have physical functions, then, when they were at 1000 level of consciousness?*

Well, Buddha had a great deal of difficulty. I only felt relieved about it when, in Korea, there was a Buddhist Bible in the hotel room. Susan was reading it, and she said, "The Buddha said he was wracked with pain and all his bones were cracked," and all. I said, "Oh, wow, that explains the whole thing." No problem. Let's see, what happened with Jesus? Well, don't forget, they have different karmic patterns. Jesus never spoke of—Jesus only spoke of enlightenment in one place. In "Matthew," he says, "Isaiah [Correction: It was Elijah] has returned to us as John the Baptist." Now, I don't know whether he meant that literally, as a reincarnation of John the Baptist, or he meant the spirit—that spirit which prevailed in Elias [Correction: Elijah] is the same spirit that prevailed. I didn't know whether he meant physical reincarnation or not, but certainly neither karma nor reincarnation and karma, as such, as a topic as understood in the Eastern world, is a subject in Christianity. Jesus Christ had no previous physical lifetimes. He never had any personal, physical human karma. As it says in the Scripture, he literally did descend from heaven. The Buddha, on the other hand, had had many previous lifetimes and recalled them with great clarity. And then, anybody who goes over 600, it's just a memory. It's not like another lifetime; it's all one continuity in which you remember being in Cleveland, you remember being in Honolulu—it's just a memory.

Q: *"Is it important for you to know what level you are, and what would be the most important thing to do each day to either maintain or increase your consciousness?"*

In describing these levels, you can pretty much guess where you are without using kinesiology. You can tell what are the devils that besiege you, you see. What is the primary emotionality? What is your view of yourself and what is your view of God pretty much tells you where you are, you know what I mean? "God hates me, I'm depressed all the time; I hate myself; I can hardly get out of bed in the morning"—well, you're about 50, aren't you, right? On the other hand, "I am in love with life; I hate to waste time just being asleep in bed; I can't wait to jump up at 4:30 in the morning; and I'm in love with nature, animals, and every animal I see. I just love it." You have to control yourself, because that does happen. Luckily you don't run into any tigers, because you would probably hug the tiger! You can pretty much know where you are. It's sort of academic interest, you know, like this audience is obvious, without even calibrating it, in the mid-400s. People who attend a thing like this are usually quite erudite and are already pretty knowledgeable and pretty well intended. You know, to take out a whole day out of your time and devote it—people who are not interested in enlightenment really are not going to blow all day when they can be watching baseball on TV, or something.

Divinity and the Self

What happens with those who cling to fear, guides and teachers, and so forth? I have not known many people like that. You know, when you speak of visions, divine entities, hearing God's voice—it's not within my experience. You see, because Divinity, that which is God, is not different than the Self. So, who would there be to speak to whom? In other words, in duality there's a "this" and a "that." There would be a "this" being spoken to by a "that." That is not the experience that has been here. There is no "this" and a "that." There is no "other" to speak to "this." The advancing awareness—because the awareness does advance from 600 on up. Astonishing things just come out of the blue, is coming from within. It's a knowingness. It's like a cauliflower that's grown a new thing. It's coming from itself—it's not of a different essence. That which grows out of the cauliflower is just the essence of cauliflower-ness. It's not an "other-ness." It's not like a beanstalk creates a cauliflower, see. So, with nurturance and for some karmic reason, that awareness, that knowledge-ness, that knowingness—the realization is one really of comprehension, the capacity to how to contextualize it so that you can say it. It doesn't change the reality of that which you are or that what you are experiencing as the Self, because that is total and complete. It doesn't need any understandings.

To be, however, committed to teaching, then is the capacity to be able to fluently language that and explain it, see. So, comes the awareness. Jesus Christ never spoke of previous lifetimes, because he never had any. That was just a knowingness. "The Buddha, however, did, resist." (True.) Isn't that fascinating—the fact that there are multidimensions, multiheavens. So, all the people you think are on mistaken pathways, you can quit worrying about them. They're all going to heaven. Yeah. There is Valhalla; there are all these heavens. If a kamikaze pilot does it for the sake of the emperor, for the sake of truth, for the sake of the Sun God—Shintoism is the Sun God of whom the emperor is the divine representative. If he is doing it for the divinity of God as represented in Shintoism by his emperor, then why shouldn't he go to an integrous place? He did it out of integrity, right? We might say he's mistaken. We might say that the Islamic terrorists are mistaken; I don't know. I never checked where they're going to go. They didn't tell them that the 72 virgins are all 900 years old! That joke came out of the blue also. I didn't make that joke up. People say, "Did you make that joke up?" No, I'm riding along the highway, and all of a sudden, it cracks me up. So, they happen of their own. I have nothing to do with them!

So, innocence is the big hole in the wall where the wolf gets in via the sheep's clothing. It is the one that the Luciferic and the satanic both use. It's because of man's not knowing truth from falsehood that he's vulnerable. See, mankind thinks he's the software; actually, he's the hardware. But he has no protective circuit that can differentiate. He puts in the software, and there's nothing that goes, "Beep, beep, beep, beep—falsehood!" No. Whatever the software, this sounds as good as this software. All software sounds good; otherwise it wouldn't sell. So, one reason that enlightenment is statistically rare is because, first of all, you have to have an intense commitment; there has to be a certain karmic setup for it; you have to have had the good fortune to run into good teachers. You have to have fallen into the soup and found a way out! This entity fell into the soup, painful soup. To get to the pits of hell, you've got to make some big errors. Karma, being throughout time, some bad decisions.

So, integrity is what carries us through. In business and spiritual work, our intention is what carries us through. It doesn't mean we won't make mistakes, but it's very difficult to make the whole trip, and even the best teachers don't forewarn some of their students about what happened. They just notice there are not as many there the next week. They don't tell you what happened to them! "We had eighteen last week, fourteen this week . . . what happened to the other four guys?"

Does the Map of Consciousness® work for after this life, in an afterlife? That's another lecture: death and the afterlife. We said that that which is Infinite and manifests itself as all the universes is like a gigantic electromagnetic field, in which through spiritual intention, it's as though you set the polarity and charge on the little iron filing we call your "self" or your "spirit." And its afterlife is automatically the consequence of what it has become by virtue of the power of the field. That's why the judgment of God is perfect. Nothing is where it should not be, because it can *only* be where it is by virtue of what it is. Therefore, a cork in the water is exactly where it is, based on its buoyancy.

Our research shows that the average consciousness advances five points in a lifetime. You know what it takes to go through one lifetime? All the agony, pitfalls, pains, contrition, penance, God-knows-what-all, it takes to go five points. At the same time, within a certain field of consciousness, certain information becomes like catalytic. I like "catalytic" because it isn't just what a thing calibrates at, but its quality. You know, its quality. And some information is catalytic—to just hear it, changes it. If you know that the time of your death is set, you can say, "I'm going to quit worrying about it." It's a relief just to know that—to know there are multiple heavens, you don't have to be afraid, "Gee, maybe I am studying the wrong teacher and I will end up in the wrong place." No, there are heavens for everybody. Because intention is what sends it. Krishna says that in the Bhagavad Gita, does he not? Krishna says, from the viewpoint of the Supreme, he was at 1000. He said, "Those that worship me, even though they are mistaken and call me by other names, by virtue of their devotion will be one with me." So, that made me feel better when I read that. That the infidel, even though—I mean, this one calls this other one "infidel" by the purity of their devotion to that which they consider Divine. So, the devotion to that which one considers Divinity Itself is sufficient guarantee to become one with the Supreme. So, that's a comforting notion. I believe in sharing that which is comforting and also sharing information where the edge of the cliff is where the edge of the cliff is.

Part II

POSITIONALITY AND DUALITY: TRANSCENDING THE OPPOSITES

CHAPTER 4

THE NATURE OF
CONSCIOUSNESS

The reason we are here is to share what we've learned about our investigations about the nature of consciousness. This is the only place I know of that is actually doing spiritual research, as amazing as that may sound. There's archaeologic research on religious history, and for that you need a little pick and a pith hat, and you go out in the desert and you hope to find something. But that doesn't really advance human knowledge.

So, what's unique about these lectures I've done is that we've discovered a means of investigating the nonlinear domain. We've found a means of investigating that which is unknowable by ordinary means. And I share with you my own experiences as consciousness advanced throughout this lifetime, and my own awareness of reality as I experience it. So, it's both subjective and, in terms of the world, objective in that we have discovered a means of verifying truth that's never been discovered before, which makes it a very useful tool. And we discovered that kinesiology itself made a very incredible tool available to almost everyone—if they calibrate over 200 and their partner does, and their question is over 200, their results are valid. We didn't even know that when we wrote *Power vs. Force*. We said we thought anybody could do it. And then I would get letters from people that they were unable to make it work. And they were trying to find out to get even with their mother-in-law or make money on the stock market—it could be the intention behind those things. But I began to suspect that, and then we discovered that the question needs to be integrous. The intention is what really sets the calibratable level of consciousness. The two people involved both need to be above 200, so it works therefore only for about 15 percent of the population, which I didn't know when I wrote *Power vs. Force*.

The discovery was that kinesiology was asking a question of the field of consciousness. Consciousness registers only that which is; consequently the other error in *Power vs. Force* is, I said it was true versus false. The correct explanation of the phenomenon is it's either true or not true. So, because that which is real exists, then that which is real registers within the field of consciousness. That which is unreal, that which the world calls false, has no independent existence, does not register in consciousness, and therefore gives you a weak response and in terms of the world, a no. We said it's more analogous to electricity going down a wire. When electricity is there, it's on. When the electricity is off, it's not on. But there is no independent existing thing such as "off-ness." That's an important point to get—there is no such thing as "off-ness." And we'll get to that more later in the lecture.

Transcending Positionality

The ego is based on a whole series of positionalities of increasing elaboration. So, we'll talk about the structure of the ego, its origin, how it expresses itself in the human domain, and how to therefore transcend it. A great deal of information itself is transformational. To merely hear certain things already resolves the problem. "It's not going to rain today"—that takes care of that one right there; you see what I'm saying? One worry just got eliminated! So, certain information itself is transformational because it's so powerful, and if you calibrate the levels of certain pieces of information, you'll see why they are so powerful.

Everything now occurs—we can start with the paradigm of context and content. Crucially important to understand that what the ego experiences is content and what Enlightenment is concerned with is context—that God is the ultimate, infinite context.

And that all of existence is then content. All that exists is content. And nothing comes into existence except for context. Therefore, God is the Source of all existence. All that exists arises solely as a specific creation of God. We explained that when we were differentiating evolution from creation. That, contrary to the ego's thought that causality works like a series of billiard balls, on the contrary: every single moment, because of creation, all that exists, its existence is because it is simultaneously and in every moment being created by God. So, God doesn't hit ball A and then go through all the next 14 balls until it comes out at the end, which is the traditional idea of the evolution of evolution. On the contrary, each and every movement of each and every ball is an individual creation of God. God creates this; God creates this; God creates this; God creates this; God creates this, so that the Creator is continuously present. So that all that is happening is a continuous creation which seems to be sequential because it's perceived sequentially. Perception is not causality.

I thought we'd start with an easy one, so we start with the simple awareness that the Unmanifest is the Godhead. In other words, out of apparent nothingness, the Buddha's Void, the Buddha Nature is the Unmanifest, having no form. Let's see if the Unmanifest is the Buddha Nature: "We have permission to ask this, resist." (True.) "The Unmanifest and the Buddha Nature are one and the same, resist." (True.) Yeah. So, this is what the Buddha was speaking of, then, because in the enlightened state, there is no form. There is no-*thingness*. There is no positionality. There is no time, space, or any point of reference. So, it seems void. But the ultimate reality is not nothingness. The error which I spoke about previously and which I wrote about more extensively in the book I am finishing now, is not to confuse the Buddha's Void with nothingness. Because, as we've said, there is no such thing as off-ness; neither can nothingness exist. One branch of Buddhism leads you into the Void. And I've been there. It's very, very impressive. It is extremely impressive. And one is certain this is what the Buddha spoke of. However, it is not. Nothingness cannot exist, any more than off-ness can exist. If we have something here, we say, "There's something here." If we take it away, you have nothingness, but you can't give me a piece of nothingness, because it doesn't exist.

So, the Unmanifest, then, is that which is prior to the universe.

One Is "All That Is"

The next realization is that one is All That Is. You can calibrate each of these levels of awareness. At the top of the chart would be a 1000 and up. As the ego disappears, there's like an agonizing shock, a feeling of literally dying. People worry about physically dying. You can forget about worrying about physically dying. There's nothing to physically dying—it's a snap, you're out of the body, it's fantastic—you wonder why you ever hung out with that stupid thing! And don't forget, 99 percent of your fears and worries have to do with the body—survival, money, health, transportation, food, eating, breathing—I mean, my God, it's really a drag. So, the minute you're out of it, you say, "Ah, this is fantastic." And then somebody shakes your knee, and it's your father, and you can see he thinks you're dead. He believes in death; you see he believes in death, and if you don't go back in the body and breathe again, he's gonna grieve. Well, if I'd been a true Buddha at that moment, I would have left it. It was his problem! I wasn't a true Buddha—it was just an enlightened state, but not the Ultimate. So, one then reluctantly re-energizes the body, which is a terrible mistake, but anyway, you do it. That was very codependent, right? We call it codependent. You agree to stay alive so your father won't grieve over your death. I mean, that's really neurotic, you know; but that's what happened.

So, in that state, in that state, one is All That Is—that Everythingness of Allness. This is Self, the awareness of reality as Allness. The Oneness and Allness, complete Totality; Infinitude beyond beginnings or endings. And in that state, one knows that That Which I Am has always existed before this universe, before other universes; when all universes have come and gone, That Which I Am is continuous, because that's experiencing God as Allness.

The state prior to that is the awareness—these are states you can reach through meditation, and we'll get into that in another lecture. When you're in meditation, you get to identify with the observer/witness rather than the content of consciousness. We should start with the dog here. The dog is barking and my leg is hurting and my name is George. And you are stuck with form. As you begin to meditate, you see that all this is going through your mind, and you say, "This is hopeless. I cannot stop the mind; it's relentless." It's thinking all the time, feeling all the time, imagining things, remembering things—it's a cacophony. It just goes on and on. So, at this point the ordinary person, as they walk around in the universe, 99.9 percent of people identify with form. That's why they're so preoccupied with health and wealth and death and all that kind of thing, because they are form and they identify life as form. The person as they start to get involved in spiritual work begins to realize that there's a step beyond that—that the mind is somehow registering somewhere. People say, "I can't stop my mind. I can't do this and that." I say, "Well, how do you know what your mind is doing? You're complaining. What are you complaining about?" Well, you must be aware of what the mind is doing, so it's registering somewhere. So, this begins to pull you back from the identification with content, and you see that something is registering what's going on in the mind. And that something is recognizing the registration of form. And then you come to the watcher.

Before you get to the watcher, you get to the experiencer. "I am George and I'm fourteen years old," or whatever, "and my dog is here." And you say, "Well, this is registering in something, because I'm recognizing it and I am experiencing it," and you begin to realize that there's a watcher of all this. There is a knower of all this; somehow there's a spotlight, there's a lens. Something is aware, and you realize that there is awareness going on, of the observer and the witness. As you go beyond the observer and the witness, you wonder, "How does . . . First of all, you begin to realize these are impersonal. You realize that observing and witnessing are happening of their own. There is no "you" that is watching and witnessing, although in the beginning, you have the illusion that's you that's watching and observing, except that you then begin to notice it does it all the time without being asked. So, if it was you, you could control it. You could stop witnessing, you could stop watching, you could stop observing. But you begin to realize that this is happening of its own, and you disidentify with that and you see that that is coming out of Consciousness itself.

As you see, you progressively let go identifying with content, and you're progressively expanding and identifying with context. The lower levels are very specific, very restricting, and completely content when you're ignoring the context altogether.

As you move up, you begin to relinquish your identification with content, and you begin to realize that that which you are is context. It is because of consciousness that any of the lower states can occur in the first place. The reason you realize they're not you is because you have no control of them, and you see they're happening spontaneously. Consciousness is there in and of itself, without being asked. You can become unconscious of consciousness when you go to sleep. And that's the oblivion! That's not the Void, that's oblivion. And many people like oblivion. And why do they like oblivion? Because it's so peaceful and happy. Well, how do you know it's peaceful and happy? So, you weren't oblivious, you were aware that it was peaceful and happy, and you said to everybody how well you slept last night. So, something is aware. Anyway. And so, we move up these levels and realize that that's where we are: at the top.

The value of kinesiology, then, is that it affirms that which has existence, that which is true, and for the first time in human history, it gives us a means of differentiating truth from falsehood. The discovery that you can differentiate truth from falsehood anywhere in time about anything is so mind-boggling that I don't think anybody on the planet has grasped the significance of it . . . including myself. It sort of blew me away for some years. And a number of people, when they first read the manuscript for *Power vs. Force*, went to Europe for a couple of weeks to just recover from the shock of discovery. That for the first time in human history, mankind has some means of navigation other than credulity—in other words, other than faith in others. Mankind has some means of telling truth from falsehood.

Calibrating the History of Mankind

When you look at the history of mankind, it's a disaster. If you don't think so, watch the History Channel a couple of nights, and it will change your mind. Well, the consciousness of mankind, you know, was about 190 for many, many centuries. And 87 percent of the population, or 85 percent, calibrated below 200. And therefore, such things as the current situation in the Middle East is the way the whole world has been. Not just the Middle East; the whole world's been that way. All of Europe was ravaged by one horde after another. All of Asia was ravaged by one horde after another. It was just one civilization plundering and savaging another civilization, continuously. And it goes on, right up to this very day. It hasn't changed at all.

Very interesting, isn't it?

So, we see the evolution of life. In the book *I* that I'm finishing up, we're trying to track the evolution of consciousness as it appeared on the planet and then evolved throughout time, on up to the present day. I am trying to recapitulate life in all of its expressions, especially as consciousness and all of life throughout all of time has evolved on this planet.

But you see that life appeared out of the unmanifest becoming manifest. And the light of consciousness then shone forth, and creation arose out of the unmanifest as the manifest. So, God as unmanifest is infinite potentiality. Therefore, the infinite context of all of creation is unmanifest; the context is infinite. The capacity of the unmanifest is beyond man's imagination, and no writer has really gotten what it is. The unmanifest has the capacity for creativity. It's innate to its nature. And all that it creates has within it the nature of that which created it, so that creation is continuous and infinite. Therefore, we tend to think of the Creator as creating this world. The more sophisticated person thinks of the Creator as creating our universe, the infinite universe. But beyond this universe is an infinite universe of universes, each of which is, at faster than the speed of light, creating an infinite series of universes. "That is so, resist." (True.) Out of an infinite series of infinite universes are arising simultaneously, faster than the speed of light, infinite universes, continuously. Therefore, that sort of expands one's concept of the Creator. Nothing comes into existence without having come from God. Nothing within the physical domain has within it "power." It has within itself only that expression in form that we call "force." Nothing that exists has the power to create its own existence. Nothing that exists has within it the power to create its own existence. All that exists arises from God.

Out of the Unmanifest arises the light, the light of consciousness with its infinite power interacting with matter, and we have life united with matter. Yeah? And creation as we know it, then, is the lighting of matter by the light of consciousness as life. The life then evolved on this planet through very rudimentary forms. It did not occur spontaneously as a happy, accidental combination of chemicals, as sort of pedestrian science would have you think. Don't forget, science is on different levels too, and what people think of as science varies all the way from the somewhat stupid to the brilliant. Just because it's labeled "science" doesn't make it mean that it's highly intelligent; very often, it isn't.

The lowest levels of science, then, are concrete-ism, literalism, and reductive materialism. So anyway, according to that theory of evolution, then, there's a happy combination of chemicals that began to breathe and think, which, you know, is unlikely. Why is it unlikely? Because you're mixing categories. There are two different categories of existence. Materiality has no capacity for consciousness. It's very obvious to anybody that thinks about it that for anything to evolve, it has to have a pattern. And where would this pattern arise? Well, the pattern arises in consciousness, and then it manifests in the physical domain. So, all power is within the field of consciousness, and what we see is the evolution of form. But the evolution of form is only a result, a consequence of that which is evolving in consciousness. How can we say that is? Because we see the progression of complexity and function throughout the evolution of life on this planet, from the smallest little bacteria at the bottom of the sea. The small, little bacteria begins to multiply and begins to learn. So, we see qualities of consciousness now accompanying materiality and physicality, because learning is not something that chemicals and molecules do.

The evolution of consciousness, then, as it manifests in form, we see as the evolution to higher and higher forms, and we see the complexity of form increasing. We see not only complexity of form, but we see aesthetics; the incredible beauty. If you watch the Nature Channel long enough, you're stunned by the incredible beauty and the complexity of the design and the discoveries made within the physical domain. The fish at the bottom of the sea that know how to produce electricity, they knew how to do that 500 million years ago, long before we discovered electricity.

Phosphorescence and electric eel . . . In the days of ancient Greece, they used to treat depression by taking an electric eel and shocking you with it. A certain number of people undoubtedly recovered—probably just so you don't get hit by that electric fish again, if nothing else!

As we see the evolution, what we're really seeing is the evolution of learning. And the capacity to store learning. So, you needed a brain, then, to store the learning in the physical domain. You see the evolution of life becoming more and more complex. You see sort of two trains of life. You see the train of life which lives at the cost of other life, and it reaches its maximum at the level of the dinosaur. Anything that's smaller and weaker, the dinosaur eats. It maintains its life at the cost of the life of the other. We might say that it's the height of egocentricity. The reptilian world, the world of the dinosaur, is the ultimate *me*. Fulfill *my* wants. If you wanna eat something, you kill it and eat it. If something is in your way, you knock it over—very much like preschool. In preschool you're not allowed eat the other children; they train them to eat cookies.

You see, the evolution of this level of consciousness is all egocentricity. So, when we calibrate 65, we're just calibrating extreme selfishness, huh? We're trying to differentiate good from evil here too, you see. When you recontextualize it, you see it for what it is. So, the dinosaur, then, is only interested in *me*. You might say evil is nothing but extremity of the ego, the ego as God. And you certainly see it in Stalin and Hitler. You see it in all these people that don't mind killing millions of people out there because they don't deserve to live. They have no rights—there's only *me*. The dinosaur is not concerned with the life of anything else except its own jaws. So, you see that evolution of life then coming up as rapacious, victimizing others. It has no concern for anything other than its own self. So, you might say the dinosaur is the epitome of the egomaniac: the megalomania which characterizes people like Stalin and Hitler and Milosevic and Nero and various people.

In another book I'm working on, we're doing about a thousand calibrations. We're doing all the famous people of history. It's sort of interesting to go through ancient Rome and calibrate the levels of consciousness of all the Caesars and the various people that have been on the planet. That level of consciousness, then, is rapacious. It reached its height at the level of expression in the level of the dinosaur. And then the dinosaur went down, and we saw the evolution of something else on the planet. We saw the evolution of the mammalian. We saw the evolution of that which lives without destroying other life. We see the sheep munching on the grass; we see the cow and all the domestic animals and the horse, and all. It eats that which is the product of light, plus chlorophyll and minerals, and in doing that, refertilizes the ground, which makes more grass. So, it not only does not kill other life; it takes the top off the grass, but it doesn't pull up its roots, and the grass comes back better than ever, having been fertilized with all kinds of manure. So, you see that which lives at the price of the life of others, and you see that which lives in a mutuality with other life in which the give and take is equal. The grass benefits from the cow, and the cow benefits from the grass.

You might say there's two different evolutionary lines, and one is rapacious. So, these biologic expressions, then, we see in the human ego. People feel guilt about the ego. This lecture is about transcending the opposites and positionality. So, you see the evolution, then, of animal life. What is the animal concerned about? The animal's concerned about survival. It's concerned about territoriality. It's concerned about right and wrong. It's concerned with being an accepted member of the family or the group. And we see that . . . You see, the evolution of consciousness, monkeys are smart enough to know that when another tribe of monkeys has beaten them, they retreat. Let's see: "The monkeys in the zoo, their civilization calibrates over 125." (True.) "130." (True.) "135." (True.) "140." (Not true.)

"In the wild they are over 130." (True.) "135." (True.) "140." (Not true.) They're still 140. When a monkey tribe is being vanquished by the invaders, it retreats, huh? It retreats. Well, the Germans didn't do that at the end of World War II. It was vanquished, and it went ahead and killed a few more millions of Russians and had a few more millions of itself killed. Japan didn't see that at the end of World War II—so hundreds of thousands more had to go.

That gives us some idea, then, how the ego arose. So, we can stop feeling guilty. The ego's not your enemy. It's not evil. And you have to understand it. It's hard to disassemble the ego without understanding it. Many people try to do it. They go into a nice, elated spiritual state, and then they fall back again. And they don't know why they keep falling back again. To stay there, you have to disassemble the ego, and to disassemble it is to merely understand it. To merely understand it is already to disassemble it. As you understand the ego, it's already getting weaker. By noon, yours is going to be weaker.

So we see the origin, then, of how consciousness then begins to express itself in the animal world. On one level as the voracious killer; on the other hand, it's also the benevolent mother. You don't see any love—there's no love amongst dinosaurs. Dinosaurs don't love anything. Even when they lay an egg, they walk away from it. They think it's disgusting and take off!

The Ego and the Brain

So, as this consciousness evolves, then, what happens is, structure begins to accommodate itself to the continuation of this form. And you have the evolution of the nervous system. Physicality doesn't need a brain. Consciousness needs a brain in which you store data, so as consciousness evolves, it learns. When you learn, you gotta store data. So, little computers. So, the brain and the neurons as they grow, they grow according to the function, and you see that the ego is really the evolution of the animal. Everything that you see on the playground, everything that you see on Monkey Island, everything you see on the TV news is not different than the animal. The animal is interested in survival, mating, protecting boundaries, territoriality, possession, grabbing things, hoarding things, pridefulness, bragging. It learns that instead of physically doing it, it can emotionally express it. It can blubber and cry and drag people all over, and all this.

What happens then is the forebrain—the intellect, then; the human intelligence didn't come in as a new, different kind of brain. The Neanderthal man's brain got better, and *Homo erectus* got better. The hominid as it evolved, you know, got better and better. So, what happened is, we just added a forebrain to the old animal brain. We didn't eliminate the old animal brain; the amygdala, and all these deep things that make you hate the guy who cuts in front of you in traffic, is still very active, right? Up comes the rage and the adrenaline before you even had a chance to think about it. So, the brain is structured to serve the animal. It's set to trigger. The anger comes up, the amygdala shoots up before your frontal cortex even gets a chance.

The ego, then, is selfishness, self-centered, and the animal instincts become elaborated through the intellect. Now man has an intellect, so he can extend his animal nature now in more sophisticated, extensive means. He becomes more sophisticated in its expression, but it's still nothing but the animal instinct out there. Convenience, satisfaction, storage—all these things now become more advanced in their expression, but the motivation is still that of the animal. To be better than another, to be able to beat them, to be richer, to be more admired, to be the alpha male, the alpha female in the pack; that juggling for position in small groups.

See, the difficulty with spiritual work—you know, as a teacher I am trying to jump the pitfalls, to recontextualize the ego, to see its true nature and how it arose. You don't have to feel guilty about it. You don't have to crush yourself because, "How could I have said that or made that mistake, how could I have been so cruel?" Because you are a vicious little dinosaur inside! You gotta own your animal, you own your animal, and the animal is called the "ego." And the ego is trained to think in terms of form. When the animal wants to eat something, it has to perceive, so the ego's primary mode is perception. If I'm going to eat this critter over here, I have to estimate the time it takes to get there, and my strength as compared to that animal. So, the animal now lives in a world of physicality and a concrete literality which takes its expression in the lower levels of science.

Nothing is real unless it can be measured. That is the lowest level of science. That pretty much clips its wings as far as becoming enlightened, because as science advances, it realizes that kind of thinking is why it can't get any further. And it has to look to consciousness itself. That's why we have conferences on science and consciousness.

The more sophisticated, the high end of the intellect in science, of course, is aware of advanced theoretical physics—subatomic, sub-particle physics. And the quantum reality, hmm? How does consciousness then interface with the physicality of the world? And that takes us to quantum mechanics— quantum mechanics, which reached its height in, I would say, the '30s. And even those who do not know about quantum mechanics, I would give you a lecture on it complete with all the mathematics—but it would put you to sleep—to prove it. You don't need to prove it any more than you need to prove that when you turn the key in the ignition, the car goes on.

Everybody who has ever heard of quantum mechanics realizes that there is a microscopic reality beyond the macroscopic world. The world of observation, the world of the ego, is macroscopic. However, there's something else going on in the universe, and everybody has heard of the Heisenberg uncertainty principle. So we'll just state one or two things about it that's significant. Smaller than the smallest atom, smaller than the smallest particle, smaller than the electron, smaller than the photon is a reality which has as a basic principle—uncertainty. So, Heisenberg's uncertainty principle is stated—things can exist either as a particle or as a wave. All exists as a potentiality. And the potentiality is influenced by consciousness, because the startling thing about Heisenberg's discovery was, an observation, the second time you make it, it's changed. The fact you've observed the phenomena has already changed the phenomena. You cannot observe the same phenomena in quantum mechanics twice. The mere act of observation has already changed its potentiality and its innate energy potentiality, as well as its position. Its position already changes.

We all know that intention changes results. We all know that what you hold in mind tends to materialize. We know that prayer is effective—not always the kind of prayer you want: "Oh, dear God, please hold the bus so I won't be late for my violin lesson." But we know that a maintained intention has a very powerful effect, and it's the most important thing karmically. It's the most important thing that determines the level of consciousness is intention. You might say that which we're accountable for is intention, not results. Let's see if that's true or not: "We're responsible for intention, resist." (True.) "It's the spiritual intention, the spiritual will that determines karma, resist." (True.) So, that keeps us from worrying about every little time we say "damn" and then feel guilty about it. It's the overall intention, the alignment. It's not every little wave that hits the prow of the ship. It's that you've set the compass in this degree. This is what's going to determine where you go eventually, and where you're at now, because it's all one.

So, we were tracking the origin of the ego in order to disassemble it; we noticed that its main purpose is survival within the animal world. And we don't see love evolve until the maternal. You see two emergences of love. You see the bonding of male to male in the hunting pack, and you see the maternal. And then you see the bonding of the maternal as nurturance.

However, we do see love evolving as companionship and friendship and play even in the early mammalian kingdom. And anybody who watches the Animal Channel sees that. Last night there was a very funny one about a parrot and a cat, I think, that bonded with each other, and they played with each other endlessly and rolled around. So, you see the evolution of love. We didn't see it in the dinosaur; the dinosaurs don't really kid around. But we do see the evolution. So, the capacity for play which then evolves through the intellect as humor.

And one of the most healing modalities useful in spiritual work is a sense of humor. I always say, never trust a person who does not have a sense of humor. They will turn you in. They're deadly. Yeah. Every whistleblower is grim. We wanted to ask about the elephants: "A group of elephants calibrates over 180." (True.) "185." (True.) "190." (True.) "192." (Not true.) Elephants are about 192. Very interesting. They have a lot of awareness and nonverbal, nonstructured awareness. There's an awareness that they *are.* So, let's see what that says: "The elephant realizes it *is,* resist." (True.) Hmm. "It realizes that others *are,* resist." (True.) The capacity to recognize existence, huh? The capacity to recognize existence. So, that awareness is why I can't hunt. And I can't see anybody really hunting who is conscious, because . . . I remember my father saying that one time, to be one of the boys, he went hunting with a .30-caliber deer rifle. And he finally discovered this deer in the woods, and he looked in the deer's eyes, and in that instant, he couldn't kill it. He saw what it was. He saw the consciousness shining out of the deer. The deer loves its life and is aware of its existence the same as you, no different at all. It just doesn't call itself "deer." But he saw that it was really existence itself coming forth as awareness of existence, and he couldn't kill it. So he never killed anything. I've never killed anything either. This is because you're aware that it loves its life. All that exists loves its life to the same degree that you love your life. Let's see if that's so: "The deer loves its life to the same degree that we love ours, resist." (True.)

So, you see, the Buddha said, and so did Jesus, that the basic problem is ignorance. See, we're trying to transcend good and evil by understanding the ego, how it arose, how it functions, how it expresses itself. You see the absurdity of life in its various apparently self-destructive expressions.

Moving Beyond Positionality

Now we wanna get beyond positionality. This is from a book I am working on now. So, we said what the ego does, then—it takes a positionality. It says everything on this side is good, everything on this side is bad, but it changes its positionality. So, what's good or what's evil then doesn't exist independently of itself, any more than "offness" exists in a wire or that "falseness" exists. It's very obvious that nonexistence doesn't exist. That may sound superficial, but it's very profound, yeah . . . I think it's profound. All right, so let's see how this works.

LINEAR GRADATIONS

Example 1 Degrees Fahrenheit	Example 2 Value	Example 3 Goodness	Example 4 Light
3,000	Precious	Heavenly	Blindingly bright
2,000	Valuable	Very good	Very bright light
1,000	Worthwhile	Good	Bright
500	Asset	Pleasant	Very strong light
100	A+	"Okay"	Light
50	Neutral	Sort of "okay"	Subdued light
0	Unattractive	Fair to middling	Dim
-50	Hindrance	Not too good	Dusk
-100	Awful	Unsatisfactory	Dark
-200	Ugly	Bad	"Pitch black"
-etc.	Repulsive	Wicked	
		Horrible	
		Ghastly	
		Horrific	

You can see that we can take any point anywhere here on the chart. This is light. We can say that light is either there or it is not there. Languaging, however, takes a point here and says, "Well, this is light and this is dark, and they're opposites." As you can see, they are not opposites; they're only a matter of degree. And the only thing I really want you to get out of this today is: there's only one variable in reality, only one. The mistake of the ego is to think there's two. Two, and those two are opposites, and that you have to choose between the opposites—good and evil, and right and wrong, and all. There's many varying degrees. Light is profoundly present, or it diminishes less and less. And when it's completely absent, we call that "darkness." Then, in languaging in the dualistic style of the ego, we say they're the opposites of light and dark. Opposites of light and dark. As you can see, they're not opposite— light is either present or not present, and it's present to a varying degree. We'll go back briefly over the levels of consciousness and see again how that works.

We can take things as far as their desirability, and we'd say, "Wow, this is heavenly; this is very good; this is sort of okay; this is fair to middling; this is sort of lousy; this is horrible; this is terrible." Right? That's degrees of desirability. But again, you see that there's no really "good versus bad"; there's only a matter of degrees. And then, conventionally in human society, we sort of mutually agree that we will call this level of light "dimness," so we label it, but the label doesn't have any actual positionality itself. We see that all definitions, then, are optional definitions for pragmatic usefulness, but there are no opposites. To merely see that takes you beyond the polarity of the opposites, which is one of the great blocks to the evolution of consciousness and spiritual work. To label anything near the bottom as "bad," "awful," "you shouldn't indulge" . . . you see, if you label a thing this side down, you're going to call it "bad," "evil," "wicked"; "We should kill it," "I should do penance."

So, we wanna just recapitulate how this translates, you see, because this is the conventional Map of Consciousness® in *Power vs. Force.* But you see that here, again, you don't have goodness versus evil—these are descriptive terms. That they are not opposites. They're all matters of degree. Matters of degree of what? They're all matters of degree of the presence of God as Love. That which is beyond all form, the context out of which we all arise, is over 1000, but when it hits human consciousness, usually we calibrate it about 1000. So, this is either the presence or the absence of love. Down at the bottom, we get more to the dinosaur. What's so sad about the dinosaur is, in human expression, it takes disdain for others—disdain for others. You know, Hitler said that at the end of World War II, "All the Germans deserve to die, because they lost the war." In fact, he was gonna burn down all of Germany, and only a few remaining generals that he hadn't assassinated—there were a few left—refused to carry out his order. He also was going to burn down Paris and destroy the Eiffel Tower. And again, his generals refused. So, there were a few sane people that realized that he was quite psychotic. So, there was a walking dinosaur in human form.

We see there are no such things as opposites—that an opposite is an artifact created by an arbitrary positionality. You can choose to call this level "rich," this level "poor." That's why government statistics—you know, the percentage of poor below the poverty level—depends on what you set the poverty level at, you know what I mean? And those are a matter of many gradations, expectations—what you set the poverty level at then decides on what percentage of the population is. When I first came out to Sedona, I had a truck full of my old tools from my tool room, and I went to the dime store and I bought a cot. And then I found an old box—that was the table, and I put a candle on there and a book, and I was home. And I lived that way. I never even closed the doors. Animals and birds blew in and out. And, you know, was I poor? I don't know. If I needed two candles and only had one, then I'd be poor, right? And I got silverware. I went to garage sales, so I got silverware for like 50 cents, and plates for a dollar, and I lived that way for a long time. If you don't need anything, you don't have any shortage. And if you don't have any needs and you don't have any shortage, you can't experience poverty.

So, there I was with nothing at all, and rich. Then I needed some cash for something; I forgot. So I had my old truck. Sedona at that time—this is the mid-'70s, late '70s; people were into gardening, but there was no manure. I discovered down in a nearby town eight miles away, there was a dairy farm with 600 head of cattle. Boy, they had a lot of manure. They heaped it up with big maw things, and then it dried. They had tons of manure. For 10 bucks they would take this thing, lift it up, dump it into the back of your truck—boom, I had a whole truckload—the back of the truck goes down. For 10 bucks I had a whole load of manure, and I drove it to Sedona and sold it for 55 dollars. Forty-five bucks cash, profit—minus the gas for eight miles. So, now I was well fixed. Before, I wasn't in poverty, but now I was pretty well fixed—45 dollars!

On the other hand, back east, I can remember a time when, if I didn't have like $25,000 by Monday, I was going to lose this and that. So, you see, poverty is where we want it to be.

Quality and Context

But there's an important point. These are not opposites; these are not the opposites of good and evil, but there is an important point. We notice, if we take the temperature of water, we need a thermometer. Here's either the presence of heat or its absence. Heat and cold are not opposites. Cold's not the opposite of heat. You can call all this hot, you can call it hot down as far as you want. Minus 50 degrees, an Alaskan might say "Boy, it's hot today." In Antarctica, this would be warm, wouldn't it? Minus 50. But we begin to notice something different happens, and that is a change of quality. We notice at this point, water turns into ice. We notice something critical here, which is that it changes quality. They're not opposites, but there is a major shift of quality. Here at 200, we notice, above 200 you go strong with kinesiology; below 200 you go weak. Above 200, you nurture life; below 200, you destroy it. Ah. So, they're not opposites, but there certainly is a major change of quality. That is the error of the politically correct person, is that they don't get that because of a shift of context. Now the context is different. Content—the meaning of content depends on context, huh? What's acceptable legal procedure during peacetime changes markedly the minute . . . ? The instant after Pearl Harbor, all of it changed. So, the context then changes the meaning of content, what's appropriate. You have to change content then, because its meaning is dependent on context.

It's politically naive to pretend that content does not change with context. Context is what gives content its meaning in the first place. So, we notice here on this calibrated level that at 200, there is a change of quality. Water, at 32 degrees. So, if we take water, below 32 degrees Fahrenheit, it's a solid. Above 32, it turns into water. Above 212, it turns into a gas. Those are very profound changes due to shift of context. Technically, the content hasn't changed, it's still H_2O. It's still H_2O, but you can't pretend H_2O at minus 30 degrees is the same as H_2O at 32 degrees, and you can't pretend it's the same at 212 just because it's still H_2O. So, that is the basis of political naivete and philosophical ignorance, and really sort of academic sophistry is the failure to realize that the quality changes—and the quality is profoundly important in a world of form.

So, here at 200, then, we have a critical shift of quality that is occurring without their becoming opposites. The fact that there's a shift of quality does not mean that they're opposites. H_2O is still H_2O whether it's solid, liquid, or gas. So, we can't say the dinosaur is evil. They calibrate down here. Their quality is considerably different because they're below the line. That which is above the line nurtures and supports life. That which is below the line is destructive of life. To see that all discernment, then, is a matter of positionality. All description is arbitrary. No such thing exists in and of itself.

So, you see then how life is evolving in varying degrees. We see that consciousness is really the appearance of love and the evolution of love. And you see almost a resistance to the lower energies, their dominance of life on this planet, almost in conflict with those that have a higher energy. It's almost like a battle to see who's going to dominate the planet. And of course, in 1986, what we discovered was that the consciousness level of mankind for the first time went over 200, and the prognosis, then, for mankind is considerably different. 190 means that eventually, man would destroy himself. My prediction was that man was going to destroy himself; it was almost inevitable. In fact, the mechanism was already in place. You remember the Russian superbomb, that if they lost the war would destroy all of life on this planet for thousands of years and millennia to come. So, the megalomaniac almost won this planet—came very close, very close. But then what happened is, consciousness went over 200. I think it's currently still at 207. Somebody asked me, has it changed since 9/11? I don't think so: "Consciousness level of mankind—we have permission to ask that in the public, resist." (True.) "It is over 206." (True.) "207." (True.) "208." (Not true.) Still 207. All right. It stayed very, very low for thousands of years and then suddenly jumped to 207. The prognosis for mankind is completely different. 207 is a whole different universe than 190.

The Western world as we know it tends to calibrate in the 400s. There's places, whole continents that calibrate maybe 70, in which disease and death and all such things are prevalent and the average age of death is 26, 29 or 30, or whatever.

So, we see consciousness then breaking forth in greater evolution primarily in spots on the planet. America is about 431, I think, isn't it? "America as we know it is over 400." (True.) "420." (True.) "430." (True.) "431." (True.) "432." (Not true.) 431, it's right on, where America is. That's quite a contrast with 70, you understand? It's a different world. We cannot judge countries that are at 70, when we're at 431. Right? You understand? It's a different world. It would be like saying alligators are wrong to eat other living things in the swamp. That which lives in the swamp, lives in the swamp and lives by the laws of the swamp. You understand how we're transcending good and evil, good and bad, wicked and . . . so, what we're trying to do this morning is transcend that positionality. The most difficult one for most people in spiritual work is good versus evil, huh? That's the one that people get hooked on, either in condemning others, which then puts them in the same point of self-judgment, or in judging themselves, which they then project onto the world and judge the world, yeah?

Positionality and Pragmatism

So, it's hard to watch the evening news without good and evil coming up, and the president of the United States, of course, has a very black-and-white idea of good and bad, and pragmatically, it works. When you're out in nature, there's certain things you'd better avoid, and then there's other things that are useful, right? So, a workable pragmatism, then. For our purposes, then, good and evil are different than what the president is saying. He's saying from a political point of view. He's also probably quite personally moralistic about it too. He probably believes that. But the spiritual aspirant has to forego that convenience. It's just a convenience. We need to just classify everything above as "good" and everything below as "bad," you see. But the backfire of that is that you then get stuck in that duality yourself. And spiritual work means giving up judgmentalism. Judgmentalism means to transcend perception. And what that means is that you have to see it differently. That means you have to contextualize it differently.

So, what we've been trying to do is to recontextualize all of life as it evolved throughout all of time, how it presents itself in various gradations so as to transcend the positionality so you don't get stuck in the duality of the opposites.

Somebody asked how the spirit energizes the body. There is a disinterest in the body as you disidentify with the body, which can happen very rapidly. I always tell people, if you're into serious spiritual work, make sure that some other people know about that, you know. Because people can think they're far from the truth, and then suddenly without warning—it comes on without warning—you're in a completely different dimension, and the physicality is actually of no interest whatsoever. Maybe it's advisable not to have people know what you're up to. I don't know. Without other people, you'd never bother with the physical body. It would just topple over eventually. So, happily, if you have people in your life that care about the continuance of that physicality, they remind you to eat and all the things that you need to do to keep it going, but left to your own devices, you'd never bother with it.

As a spiritual aspirant, there's nothing to worry about, because once you're a spiritual aspirant, you've already committed to, we said, the Spiritual will. In meditation and all spiritual work, the field seems to be scattered. You look at the content of consciousness, you look at the mind and events of the world, et cetera. Your life seems sort of scattered, and that's sort of worrisome. First, "I'm reading this book," then "I'm reading this book; then I'm seeing this guru, and then I'm going to that lecture." But one's spiritual commitment—so, the decision of the Spiritual will is what determines karma, karmic consequences, and determines the fate of the spirit.

One Karmic Unity

The entire universe is one karmic unity. Everything within this universe is related to everything else within this universe, based on the laws which are of the nature of the Creator. Because the entire universe comes from one creation, therefore, the entire universe is one karmic unity. Nothing is beyond the karmic oneness of all of creation. Consequently, whether people believe it or not is irrelevant, that one's destiny is already karmically determined. Even if when you die, you go into oblivion and there's nothing more, that's already karmically determined, isn't it; you didn't determine that. So, even though people deny karma, that's just a conceptual thing that they're talking about. What they mean by karma, when people deny karma, what they mean is reincarnation. Well, reincarnation is one thing; karma is another. We're going to do a lecture on that, so I won't go into it extensively here. But as we demonstrated, I think, in a previous lecture, Jesus Christ never had any previous physical lifetimes. He never spoke of any previous lifetimes. One reason is, he never had any, heh heh. Interesting, eh? The Buddha, on the other hand, had many previous lifetimes, and the Buddha spoke of it extensively. The Buddha remembered many previous lifetimes. I myself remember many lifetimes in great detail. Let's just ascertain the truth of that: "Jesus Christ never had any previous physical incarnations, resist." (True.) That's correct. "The Buddha had many, resist." (True.)

So, Jesus, one reason he didn't speak about previous lifetimes and reincarnations is, he never had any. And by questioning, we got that Christ did come down from Heaven, that dominion, that domain, and did incarnate and never had a previous physical lifetime. The Buddha, on the other hand, evolved through countless lifetimes, and so their teachings are different. Christ came for salvation. Christ teaches salvation. Buddha teaches enlightenment. Again, don't confuse the two; they're two different things. Enlightenment is one thing; salvation is another.

Questions and Answers

Q: *"How does spirit function practically in the physical body?"*

Spirit doesn't really function. Spirit is like the electricity in the wire, and the electricity doesn't care what form that flows into it. It could be a toaster oven; it could be a microwave. It doesn't really care, because it only is what it is. It doesn't change function. So, the spirit, then, you might say, is the energy of life itself. The energy of life itself. It manifests depending on the form in which it finds itself.

Q: *"How do you calibrate truth versus non-truth if you don't have a partner to do kinesiology?"*

That's a frequent question. And a lot of people know this particular technique, the O-ring, where truth makes you go strong and you can't break the ring. So, that's one technique you can use on your own. There's many people who know how to do it. If you go on the Internet, under "kinesiology" there's quite a list of resources. Also, from the levels of consciousness, you can pretty much guess where you're at and where everybody else is. If this is a meritocracy, where a college education and intelligence, reason and logic, and science—the new god of the world is not religion, but science—and then you can pretty much know, you can guess America is in the 400s; you don't really have to calibrate it. So, if you really look at the levels of consciousness and you see what prevails, you can pretty much guess the level of consciousness.

The Healing Effect of Letting Go

The letting go of negativity in all the forms in which you can, tends in and of itself to have a healing effect. The letting go of judgmentalism . . . I always tell anybody in the office who has any kind of affliction, "If you haven't done the Course in Miracles, you ought to do it before you die from what you've got!"

The *Course in Miracles* is very, very practical if you've got cancer, high blood pressure, whatever ails you. I did original research on them when it first came out. I knew the authors; I knew Helen and Bill, and all those people. And we had an Attitudinal Healing Center at my clinic back east. We had the second one. Jerry Jampolsky started the first one in Tiburon. And he and his crew came out and stayed at my house. Back east I had a very large house. And we spent the weekend, and we started the second Attitudinal Healing Center. The purpose of the Attitudinal Healing Center was to practice the principles of the *Course in Miracles*, no matter what the ailment was. So, we had people with multiple sclerosis, all kinds of illnesses. I've seen every kind of illness that walks the planet remit, go into remission and heal itself. And the Institute of Noetic Sciences has records, proven medical records of something like 86,000 miraculous cures and healings from every affliction known to mankind.

We notice that when you're at a certain level of the lessons, you're only subject to what you hold in mind and you can begin to deny, refuse and release it, and recover from it. And all the ailments I had when I took the *Course in Miracles* all disappeared.

No matter what other spiritual work you're doing, do the *Course in Miracles* because, first of all, it's hysterically fun. I mean,

I'll never forget the first lesson. Here I am, a psychiatrist, and the lesson is, "Nothing your mind thinks means anything." I almost fell off the toilet, it was hysterical! I mean, I recognized the genius of it—this is genius. Instantly, I saw the genius of it: nothing your mind thinks means anything. So, the *Course* is beautiful. And, you know, Science of Mind, the 12-step groups, and the *Course in Miracles* are all beautiful ways of transcending the negatives and putting you in a very good place. All of them will take you into the high 500s. Alcoholics Anonymous calibrates at 540. The *Course in Miracles* calibrates at 600. So, to get out of the bottom of the box and transcend to higher levels . . . The purpose of Christianity is really to reach 540. I mean, what Jesus Christ taught was designed to get you to 540, which is Unconditional Love—to pray for your enemies, to turn the other cheek, et cetera. To give up hatred and pray for them, to see them as ignorant rather than evil. That's all designed to get you to 540. And from 540 on, anybody who reaches 540 has no worries in this universe, because 540 is Heaven and beyond, and 540 is also, I think, the Lotus Land of Buddhism. I never calibrated Lotus Land, but I think it would calibrate about the same: "Lotus Land is about 540, resist." (True.) Okay.

So, the Buddha, you see—Buddhism has various schools also. And Lotus Land Buddhism envisions the Buddha—who then has a different name because his function is different as the Buddha of salvation—that there is a certain understanding that the negativity of this world is so severe that the average human is unlikely to reach Enlightenment from this plane. That it's like the gravity here is so strong that to transcend the level of gravity of the consciousness of this world is so unlikely that it's better to be practical; aim for 540, which is Heaven. And from Heaven you don't have to worry, because Heaven at 540 is beyond the tremendous gravity of so much negativity. So, in that function, the Buddha stands for the savior: he's the Buddha of salvation and the Buddha of Lotus Land Buddhism. So, Lotus Land Buddhism and Christianity are very practical, very practical. Reach 540 and you don't have to worry, because from there on, the Great Beings will lift you and you'll be okay.

So, I don't worry about anybody once they reach 540. I don't really worry about anybody once they get to 500. And I really don't worry about anybody when they're in the 400s or even the high 300s.

The Importance of Willingness

As you know, I calibrated Walmart. In *Power vs. Force*, we calibrated Walmart, and Sam Walton and I corresponded back and forth. I approved of Sam Walton because he stood for integrity, integrity. And he liked the book, and uh . . . anyway, I think we calibrated Walmart, and in those days, it was like 380 or something. Well, 350 and up is Willingness. So, when you walk into Walmart, their attitude is, "How can I help you?" Right? That's Willingness. We have friends, if you're carrying out packages to the truck, they run over and say, "Can I help you? Can I help you?" So, that's a very positive level, you know. The world at the time was 190. Here's Walmart at 370, or something. So, anyway, we predicted that Walmart would do well. And two weeks ago, I think it was announced Walmart has become the largest, most successful corporation in the world, in the entire world. So, 350 or 360 is a lot different than Enron. To be helpful, to be integrous, to give you a good product and made in America—all those things are integrous. So, integrity in the long run takes you a long way.

The *Course in Miracles* I think is based on what we're talking about this morning; in other words, to let go of a positionality, which creates a duality, which puts you in good versus evil and puts you into a polarized, dualistic belief system. So, the *Course in Miracles* is designed to transcend that belief system, take you out of perception, to a nonjudgmentalism. All right, nonjudgmentalism. So, the *Course in Miracles*, then, is based on forgiveness. In order to forgive, you have to have already made a judgment. To have made a judgment, you had to adopt a positionality. So, our purpose this morning is, in a way, the same as the *Course in Miracles*: to transcend positionality, stop seeing it as good and evil. We don't have to hate Bin Laden; we don't have to hate dinosaurs. We don't have to hate 'em. I wouldn't hang out with 'em, though, because they'll eat you alive. It doesn't mean you have to become stupid—it just means that you have to comprehend that which you experience from a different context. And spiritual work is really one of identifying with a more and more diffuse context, getting away from the specifics of content. We're going to do a lecture later on meditative techniques, and there's a meditative technique in which one focuses primarily on peripheral vision, which anybody can do. It's working in the same direction as the *Course in Miracles* or consciousness research such as we're doing.

As you walk about the world, instead of focusing on the content and the itty-bitty-nitty-gritties, you focus on the context, the overall space in which you are, the overall space and the intention for which you're in this space. In other words, you identify with the context out of which life arises. And then, of course, at this moment it's taking this form, but your identification becomes progressively less with this body and this table and this particular audience, and it eventually takes you to existence itself. So, as you let go identifying with and focusing on content, you realize that you are the context. You thought that you were the content, and you realize, "Oh, I am the context in which it's all happening, I'm the theater. I thought I was the play." Oh, you're not the play, you're the theater.

So, constantly expanding context means, then, you're less and less vulnerable to what people say and do, because they're more like in a movie, you see. This actor says this, and this actor says this, and there's no point in taking it personally, because it's all just happening in a movie and has nothing to do with you, because that which you are is the context, the awareness, and not the content. You're not the content, you know. So, the less you identify yourself as this thing here saying this thing here, you're more the witness of what's happening. You're the witness. So, you're the witness of what's happening in the Middle East; you don't have to make it right or wrong. You don't have to feel bad about it. You don't have to try and change it.

Ramana Maharshi, who's well-known to probably many of you here, said that there's no point to try to change the world, because the world you see is just a perceptual illusion; there's nothing that needs changing.

If the world is one big, huge karmic unity, then what is it you're going to do that's going to change all that? "The Palestinians and Israelis as a people want peace, resist." (True.) "The politicians involved want peace, resist." (Not true.) Politicians don't want peace. So, send a politician to talk to politicians who don't want peace, to go for peace. They've already made up their minds.

So, is that right or wrong? Neither one. Is it something we should desire or not desire? Neither one. Ramana Maharshi says, "The world you see is a projection of the ego." Which is what we're seeing this morning. So, how to then change what it is that you are projecting? So, we won't see the Middle East as good or evil; we'll see that it's not too evolved, right? It's over here someplace. It's not too far along in the evolution of consciousness.

Transcending the Opposites

To transcend the opposites of good and evil, right and wrong, is already a major spiritual advancement, because it means to let go of positionality and judgmentalism. A positionality is, after all, a judgment. The Course in Miracles says let go of all judgments, and then perception is replaced by vision. You see the magnificence and the beauty of life without projecting anything onto it. So, That Which Is, then, is beyond categorization and beyond descriptive terms. And it just stands forth in the brilliance of the Divinity of its Creator. All that exists is innately a manifestation of God. The non-form within form is the Presence of God within all of Creation. Nothing can exist otherwise. And the letting go of positionality, then, in one instant suddenly, at least in this experience—there were a number of experiences, incredibly beautiful; the snowbank with my father and the many other similar ones. But the one that happened in '65 was very sudden and unexpected, in which all becomes totally silent; and the wording and the talking that people do, which to this day I have difficulty understanding, and I have to say, "What?" many times. Because it's the silence that predominates, and the noise is . . . the noise, the words, the verbiage is in the background, and you have to focus on it and bring the verbiage in across the silence.

In ordinary life, the sound predominates. People don't notice silence, because they're hearing the birds and the talking and the movie going on, and their focus is on the sound. But, you understand, you cannot hear sound except against a background of silence. It's because of silence that you can hear sound. Without silence you can't hear any sound, for the same reason that without the emptiness of space, you could not discern an object, yeah? Without the non-form of consciousness, you would not be able to comprehend, perceive form. It's because of the formlessness of consciousness you can perceive form. It's because of the silence that you can hear sound. And in that state, one is the silence and not the sound. And people are into sound all the time. Anyway, in trying to readjust to the world, one has to readjust to focusing on sound and verbiage and meaning and all that, but it's tiring and you have to say, "What?" all the time, which makes you sort of stupid. But if people explain it, then I guess your intention to comprehend is what makes it comprehensible, you know. Otherwise it's not really comprehensible. It's because the Presence prevails as the primary reality of which you're aware.

CHAPTER 5

SPIRITUAL INTENTION AND COMMITMENT

So, when we go up the levels of consciousness, one goes up through Lovingness to willingness to surrender judgmentalism. To get to 540 is Unconditional Love. "Unconditional" means you gotta let go of right and wrong and begin to see that it's not appropriate; it's irrelevant. That's done in 12-step groups all the time, and I use the example of the guy who runs over three people, burns down a house, and goes to a meeting the next day and they say, "George, we're sure glad to see you here. You sure belong here." That's all they care about—that he's at a meeting where he needs to be. So, it means the willingness to forego judgmentalism.

The way you transcend judgmentalism is the willingness to forego it. How can you forego it? You can forego it because you see it's irrelevant. If a dog is biting your ankle, it's irrelevant whether the dog is a bad dog or not—he's biting your ankle, you know what I'm saying? This is not the time to hang out and decide whether he is a good or bad dog, you see. Whether what goes on in the Middle East is good or bad is irrelevant. It's irrelevant. So, it's really that you transcend judgmentalism because you see it's irrelevant. It's a "So what?" So, the way you transcend right and wrong and judgmentalism is, you see that it's just a "So what?" I mean, "So what?" You know what I mean? The guy was wrong when he did so-and-so. Well, so what? So, he was wrong. So? So, big deal. In other words, one gives up the trying to juice it, huh? See, what people do with right and wrong is they wanna juice it. People like judgmentalism and right and wrong-ness and morality because you get to be on the "good side" and you can juice it. You hate to say that you're better than they are, but you *know* it, see? "I hate to tell you you're wrong, brother, but you know you're wrong," you know. To be polite, you don't say it, but you know it. "He's a creep, he always is a creep."

So, the lower levels of consciousness all have their payoff. The way you transcend them, you don't have to transcend those levels of judgment. All you have to do is transcend, to say no to the payoff. And, as you let go of the payoff, they disappear. When you don't take glee in putting your thumb in somebody's eye anymore, you stop putting your thumb in people's eye. It's because you are getting off on it. "Take that, you!"

So, people, the ego, what's the ego addicted to? This is a great moment in history. The ego is addicted to the juice it gets out of its positionalities. That's what keeps it in place. It gets *off* on it.

Anytime you can get yourself into the position of victim, there is a big payoff. You get sympathy, you get attention, you get to be on Channel 15, you get to blubber all over, and you get a million-dollar lawsuit. People say, "How can I get away from all this stuff?" You can get away from it if you get the secret to it.

So, to transcend, then, the lower levels of the ego, it doesn't mean to go beyond all these things. It means to let go what you get out of it. You get a lot out of despising things; you get a lot out of hatred. Vindictive is what runs all these people. We love to condemn people, make them wrong, look down on them, laugh at them, spit on them, put them in prison, get even—there you go! Or we can put them down with ignoring them. So, it's really the willingness, and to make it coincide with the *Course in Miracles*, which many people here have done, is then to let go of the pleasure of judgmentalism. That's how you get out of it. You get off it and you let go of the pleasure because you see it's irrelevant. You see that you're trying to get pleasure out of something that has no basis in reality. When you see that it's an arbitrary positionality, you realize that it's fake. It's like trying to measure water with a ruler—it's just the wrong instrument.

Judgmentalism is just the wrong instrument to apply to human life. Why? Because human life is coming out of an incredible complexity. The evolution of consciousness and all of its karmic expressions throughout all of *time* is what accounts for this piece of dust here right at this moment. What can you say about that? Everything that you see is the result of the evolution of all that has ever been throughout all of time since the beginning of time. For a piece of dust to be here, this air has to be here, the barometric pressure has to be here, this room has to be here. Sedona has to be here; it has to be Arizona; Arizona has to be in a country; all that has to be on a globe. All that has to be in a planetary system whirling around a universe. For this globe to be here at this moment, and for the light to be where it is and the sun to be where it is, the barometric pressure—an infinite number of things has to have evolved throughout all of time to account for this particular moment. So, to be judgmental about it seems sort of inappropriate, right?

Down here on the chart, you've got apathy. You've got the old lady sitting there in the rocking chair. She stopped eating. She won't answer the telephone. She lost all interest in life. She's gonna die. You see her in the nursing home. Unless you pour energy into her, she's gonna die. Maybe these people are coming out of apathy.

If you come up to rage and angriness, you can at least move yourself out of apathy. That's the value of television. You see all those beautiful things there on TV. All the people that are into apathy: "Hey, look at what those people there have, Nellie." "You know, Pete, let's get one of them there toasters." "Well, you've gotta have money for that. That means you gotta go to work, right?" "Yeah, whittle some chairs and sell 'em, or somethin'."

Humility

So, what does "humility" mean? In spiritual work, humility is of profound importance. It means, I of myself, as an ego, am completely unable to comprehend reality. I have no way of knowing the truth of anything; much less can I discern its karma. Therefore, all judgment is up to God. Judgment is Mine, sayeth the Lord. Why? Because you're not capable of it. Not capable of it. You would have to know the totality of all of existence throughout all of time up to the point of this little piece of dust right here to explain one piece of dust, much less anything as complex as the tribal wars that have been going on in the Middle East for thousands of years and will probably continue to. Why? Because it serves that purpose. If life on earth is purgatorial, it's certainly not heavenly. If human life on this planet is an aspect of purgatory, then that which seems horrible to us, isn't it necessary? It's only when you've had enough suffering that you say, "Hey, there must be a better way." It's only because you find out that this all leads you into agony that you finally give it up, right? How does the spirit hit bottom and make a choice for God instead of worshiping itself as the ego, as megalomania, huh?

Consequently, we can't even judge the purpose of human life itself, much less anything that occurs in it. "The purpose of human life as we know it on this planet is primarily purgatorial, resist." (True.) Wow. You don't have to worry about purgatory, you're in it! Everybody who worries about purgatory makes me laugh.

So, it means, then, that karmically we've earned the right to be in a place where we have a choice, and we can determine our own destiny by the choices we make. So, the absolute benevolence of Divinity is that by one's own choice, one determines one's own karmic destiny—not some arbitrary God who hates you and throws you into hell or beats you up. Most of the religions of the world believe in a God who beats you up, you know. No, you get to determine it yourself. So, the freedom then to realize the source of your own existence is that you have infinite freedom. That infinite freedom is, there's no limits upon your choice and that you are reborn. As the Buddha said, "There is no greater thing to be grateful for. The likelihood of being born a human on this planet is extremely rare. To be born a human on this planet and to have heard of Enlightenment is rarer still. Therefore, waste no time." So, all of us here have accepted that awareness. That we're all here and we have accepted that we are spiritual beings and that choice is within in our own hands, and the freedom then to become more evolved is merely a choice.

The choice is then simplified, so we will repeat how simple it is, so that we don't look like dumbbells when we leave this planet! So, it's a simple thing, then. We give up the *pleasure* of judgmentalism, that secret little feeling of glee of your being right and the other person is being wrong. That's a hard one to let go of. So, the ego persists because it's addicted to the juice it gets out of its positions. Let's see if that's right. I never called it "addicted" before. "The ego is addicted to the payoff it gets, resist." (True.) Wow. Yes. It's addicted. Hey, we're all hooked on the ego. The ego is hooked on the juice it gets out of stuff. I mean, there's nobody juicing a thing more than a victim. You see a victim on TV, oh man, they juice it for all it's worth, man. All the melodrama and the vindictiveness and how wronged they were and how right they are and how the world owes them now. Tens of millions they're gonna get, too.

Honesty

Spiritual evolution requires honesty. What do we need to be honest about? Most people think, "Well, I need to be honest in looking at my sinful side, my negative side, my bad side." It becomes onerous. In 12-step groups they have a fourth step, and a lot of people would rather die than take the fourth step, because the fourth step is where you take a spiritual inventory—a strict, honest spiritual inventory. Most people hate Step Four. And would rather stay drunk and die than become honest about it. It's because they think they're going to have to go through a guilt trip.

So, if we recontextualize it, you don't have to fear a guilt trip in admitting spiritual honesty. What you're really going to do is, admit that the ego is an evolution from the animal world. It has all the characteristics of the animal world. It needed to do that for survival. Those survival techniques have now become elaborated into levels of human expression. Institutions, the government, the courts, the departments, the bureaus, all now serve the function that was once served by sneering in the wolf pack.

Let's do our llamas. We've got seven llamas. And the way the llamas do this—they're big, woolly guys, you know. They're very interesting, the llamas; they're adorable. Llamas have such a wonderful coat of fur that in the middle of winter, it will snow, and they've got this much snow on their backs, yeah. You come back tomorrow, and the same snow is still standing there. Hadn't even melted. The warmth of their body doesn't even get through their fur to melt the snow on their backs. It's really amazing. Well, this is the way llamas communicate. Now, if this female doesn't give in to the alpha female, she spits at her. That's why they spit. They don't spit at humans unless they're not trained right. When they're real little, you don't play with them a lot, because they think you're another llama and include you in their family pack. They then treat you as a peer and will spit at you. But if you wait until they are a year or two old before you play with them, then you're not one of them and they don't spit at you, because you're not one of them.

What's interesting about watching the world, and in the animal world especially, there is so much spiritual information in watching the Animal Channel. Because you watch, you're seeing how the ego plays itself out. And it's easy to see, because it's not you, it's them. You see? So, society, the newspapers, and the TV, and all is interesting because you see the ego displayed out there. Because it's not a personal you, it's very easy to see how it plays. You see, in your own life, it's a little harder to see how it plays, because that person deserves it—that's harder to see. But on TV, projected, you can see the ego games going on. And the ego, you know—so, human life is really the game board of the ego. The ego is just a game board. And you see, the llamas, what they're doing is this whole one-upmanship deal, you know, who's the more dominant one. And that's because they value that dominance.

I don't value dominance. Someone tells me he's got a bigger car, more money, and he's governor of the state; I think that's all interesting, but you know, I don't react to it. So, in other words, you would have to adopt that value to be competitive about it. You understand? So, as human beings we have choices the animal doesn't have. We can choose whether social status is important to us or not. At a certain point of life, it's probably pathologic that it doesn't. And beyond a certain point of life, it's pathologic if it persists. If you're young and you don't care about it, you're probably in apathy; but when you reach a certain point of life, you know, such things as status and all become rather meaningless.

Transcending the Ego

So, we transcend these things by giving up the fact that they don't have any payoff anymore. Having status and a big house and a lot of money doesn't have any payoff. When it doesn't have any payoff, you let it go. It doesn't mean anything anymore. You can walk away from it and not really feel any loss, because you've already juiced it and seen what's there, and you don't need it anymore. So, the secret, then, to transcending levels of consciousness is to just see that the ego is the residual of the animal world. It's not personal. It's built into your brain. In the back of your brain is the old reptile brain. Nothing you can do about that, folks. Wanting to kill the guy that pulls in front of you in traffic—that's normal. Any good dinosaur would chop him up and eat him! The only thing is, you're not a dinosaur anymore.

So, you see, you develop a sense of humor, a lightheartedness because you're not identifying. The value of humor—humor is a way of dis-identifying and getting distance from things. The more evolved you get spiritually, the greater your sense of humor becomes, because everything becomes ludicrous, ridiculous, and absurd when seen from a certain viewpoint, because you're not identifying with it anymore. So, the llamas out there, as they do their whole thing, are very entertaining. That's because we are not llamas. If we were llamas, we wouldn't think it was so entertaining. It would be life or death for us, right?

So, getting even, being vindictive, all those things, you only persist in them so long as you're getting a payoff. So, there's only one thing we have to surrender and let go, and that is the willingness to get the payoff of these various spiritual positions. If you're willing to let go of the payoff, then suddenly, That Which Is prevails. And the reward is 10 million times greater than anything you'll ever let go of. One instant in that Presence is worth all the pain and suffering of all the spiritual work you ever did. The knowingness that comes out of it—that one is safe forever, there is nothing ever to fear, ever again. The Reality of That Which You Are. If you're context, then you're immune to content, right? That sounds rather abstract, but if you, as you walk around in the world, realize that you're context and not content, then you realize that you're absolutely safe, because it's only as content that you're in danger at any time. The fact that the store is staying open and that you're there, and Walmart is running is not going to be changed by you and the clerk and what goes on. In other words, that which prevails continues to prevail, so you identify more with that which is prevailing than the details of it. And that takes you out of the line of fire.

And instinctively you'll know it, and a lot of times you go through diuresis. In spiritual work you find yourself building up tension and gaining weight and retaining salt. And suddenly, you reach a state of realization and, wow, you just pee up a storm for a day or two! You let go of retaining all that sodium chloride. So, you'll see the fluctuations in spiritual work, and just when you think you're not making any progress, that's the time to continue straight ahead. The one training that is of ultimate value is to "walk straight ahead no matter what." And at the front— this you need to know, because anybody doing spiritual work, you can reach the final doorway totally unexpected. You can be just muddling along, getting absolutely nowhere along, and one day you start doing some spiritual practice or looking at something, and suddenly you're looking at the infinite possibility of letting go of the sense of "I" that you're familiar with. And at that last moment, at that last moment, you need the words to "walk straight ahead." No matter what you run into in spiritual work, walk right through it, because it's all illusion. Any fear that you can come up with is illusory, because in reality, there is no fear. Consequently, to experience fear, that's an imagination of the ego. Therefore, there's no danger in walking through any kind of fear that arises during meditation.

Anybody who does spiritual work can be confronted with that last moment right before Enlightenment where the fear of letting go the sense of "I" as who I am comes up. At that moment you'll remember to walk through the fear, that you're absolutely safe. When you let go of all that you think you are, then you realize the truth of what you absolutely are, and you're beyond fear forever.

See, the reality is that everything is happening of its own. We mentioned it before. As you concentrate more and more on the peripheral, on the space in which everything is happening instead of the specifics of what's happening, you become detached from the yin and yang, the pull and the push of solar-plexus interaction of the world in which everybody is trying to manipulate a response out of you. And as you identify more with the space and as you get into the habit of that, it's like a walking meditation, and then all of sudden, you notice everything is happening of its own. Nothing is causing anything else. All is happening of its own. Everything's happening spontaneously. And everything is merely being that which it is. Nothing is causing anything. Each thing is fulfilling its potential to be what it is. That's why the bird flies. It's not *caused* to fly. It doesn't even have any purpose to fly. It just flies because that's what birds do.

We did a lecture prior on causality and the basic illusion of the ego. You don't get really beyond causality until an extremely high level, but I think it jumps. To be aware always of the space in which all is happening instead of the content of the space takes you sort of out of it, gets you out of that solar-plexus, yin-yang grasp of the world which is always trying to manipulate your emotions. And usually, it's through the solar plexus, you know, although they appeal to the spleen a lot, too.

Questions and Answers

Q: "Is the human body an indication of the belief
in separation from God?"

Well, yes and no. Yes, it is. As I said, the body evolves, as it belongs to the planet. It is part of the physical universe. The body is an evolution of the animal world. And the self, the small self, identifies with it as being separate. Did the small self think it was separate before it identified with the body? Well, yes it would have; otherwise it wouldn't have chosen a body. I mean, to say no to my father and reactivate the body was taking that chance that when you reidentify with the physicality, that you'll believe you're separate from the One. That's the risk in doing that. And generally, it's not advisable.

Q: "What actually happens when people worldwide pray for peace?"

That was the Harmonic Convergence. I said that consciousness level jumped from 190 to 207 in the late '80s. That was the time— it coincided with the Harmonic Convergence, which coincided with the time when a great many, a high percentage of spiritually evolved people on the planet all prayed for peace simultaneously. We all got up at four o'clock in the morning or something; I forget what it was. Yeah, I think it was four in the morning. And that jump occurred about that same time. Now, as I said, causality is an illusion of the ego. So, you can't say that all those people praying for peace caused it to jump to 207, nor that the Harmonic Convergence caused it to happen, or any particular alignment of the planets caused it to happen. No. It's more that something outside of all these events simultaneously brought them all into existence. So it has to do more with advanced theoretical physics understanding that the spinning electron on this side of the universe doesn't cause the one on the other side of the universe to spin. That that which is outside both of them but encompasses both of them is simultaneously . . . so, people ask me about astrology, and the alignment of the planets, of course, is a perceptual illusion. There's no alignment of the planets—it's all in your head. If you go up there in a spaceship, you're not going to see any Pegasus up there. There ain't no such animal. But it can be that that which brings on a state of peace—in other words, the two are happening simultaneously—it's not that the alignment of the planets is causing this, but that which is concordant. The blooming of flowers is concordant with the spring, you know what I'm saying?

In the book *Eye of the I*, it says—I mentioned that the book of Revelations is an aberration in the New Testament. Things that I warned as a caveat at the beginning of the book: it says that the traditionalist religionist may be disturbed by this and better read something else. The evolution of religion, you see, came out of primitive—you know, all of life came out of a primitive condition. And primitive man, when he heard thunder and lightning, as he evolved, began to think it was the angry gods. And so, we see the Incas sacrificing virgins, we see the ancient tribes of Israel, we see primitive man considering God from an anthropomorphic position. And why wouldn't he? So, we can't make man wrong for doing that. If you're primitive man and it thunders and lightnings, and all, you figure the gods must be angry, so you sacrifice a few more virgins to pacify the gods. So, the anthropomorphic images of God, of course, were common.

They're projections from the unconscious. They're also projections of the concept of causality. Of course, what man forgets is that all these catastrophes and floods and volcanoes and hail and all that went on long before mankind appeared on this planet. We've only been here 400,000 years. Well, for millions of years, all this has been going on, so obviously it's not done by an angry god to get even with man, 'cause man wasn't even here yet. So, the primitive belief, then, is that it projects its fears onto a Divinity and then imagines that they'll have to meet this Divinity, which is a projection of their own unconscious. So every culture has it. You know, we get the lord of the underworld weighing your sins, et cetera. Every culture has its primitive origins, and some persist. Some tribal belief systems still persist and are revered.

Others, paradoxically, are quite evolved. The indigenous traditional beliefs were quite evolved. Chief Detroit calibrates at 700. He gave a very famous address which is of a very high level of spiritual understanding, so the Great White Spirit of the Native American was already considerably more evolved than many supposedly more advanced civilizations. In the American Indian, you saw the divinity of all of life. That's why he prays and asks the deer for forgiveness. "I have to eat you for dinner." Well, the deer doesn't mind. The purpose of the deer's life is to give life back to the Indian. So, there's a mutuality. So, some seemingly primitive tribes had pretty advanced consciousness, and understanding that the Divine spirit is present in all that lives is a pretty advanced state of awareness.

The difficulty with Christianity considerably has been the decision to include the Old Testament with the New. The Old Testament is full of all the tribal anthropomorphic projections of God as an angry, vengeful, jealous, insecure paranoid. There's only three books of the Old Testament that make you go strong with kinesiology: Psalms, Proverbs, and Genesis. Proverbs is in the 300s, and I like Proverbs. It's full of really pithy sayings, sort of like Ben Franklin, you know. I like Proverbs. Psalms, of course, is beautiful and poetic and mystical and lovely. And Genesis comes forth with the first statement of that which man really needs to know. And that is that you're created by God. The importance of that statement surpasses everything. Why it wasn't included in the New Testament is beyond me, but anyway, historical reasons being what they are.

The difficulty with Revelations is John, who was the source of Revelations, had a—those are lower-astral hallucinations. If you calibrate Revelations, it comes out at 70; 70 is the spleen; 70 is coming from the lower astral. So, when we said this morning there's an infinite universe of universes, these universes have different dimensions. The higher and lower astrals are the most commonly known to man because man's contacted those domains through hallucinations, hallucinogenic drugs, nightmares, illusions. So mankind has been able to contact the higher astral, where there's devas and beautiful channelers of sort of angelic level and rather evolved beings. And then, of course, the dimensions in the astral go down the same as they do here. And so, you have the lower-astral realms of the demons and the devils and various no-goods.

A lot of these entities in the lower astral like to hook humans. Now, what is the lower astral made up of? The lower astral is made up of those who deny God—no, not deny God—those who *refuse* God. Because you can be a truthful atheist and agnostic, and say, "I just really don't know." That's not refusing God; that's saying honestly, "Because of the limitation of my intellect and my personal experience, I cannot get into the question one way or the other meaningfully, and therefore honestly, I decline it." I was an agnostic for many years. What was I going to say? Oh, yeah. So, the lower astral, however, is made up of people who had the opportunity and the capacity to accept God but have refused it, refused God. Okay, let's make sure if that's correct. "The lower astral is made up of those who refuse God, resist." (True.) "It is not the same as those who deny God, resist." (True.) "Those who deny God can still go to good places, resist." (True.) There's hope for everybody. There's an honest man's level of heaven where all good atheists and agnostics go. We all know people who are ethical, principled, and you'd trust them with your bank account, but when it comes to the religion and all that, they say, "I don't know; I just can't handle it."

I've got a patient like that. He's getting older and older and he knows he's going to die, and he says, "Doc, I just wish I could believe the way you believe, but I don't know; I was brought up by the Catholic Church, and somehow I just can't get over it." I said, "Well, you gotta forgive your upbringing, because it wasn't really the Catholic Church; it's the way man held religion back in the twenties and the thirties." You know, we all grew up with . . . One of the reliefs of becoming an atheist or agnostic, or whatever I was—I think I was first an atheist and then I got more sophisticated and became an agnostic—was the great relief of fear and guilt about sin, you know. And sin was a spot on your soul, my mother would say, and if you sin, you get this spot on your soul.

Oh my God! And then if you went to communion with this spot on your soul, God knows what happens. It's too awful to imagine!

The Lower-Astral Dimension

So, the lower astral is very common in Sedona. There's channelers all over, from all kinds of dimensions on the other side, God bless them. There is Baba this and Baba that on the other side and all kinds of controllers and trans-mediums. It's something I warn about in the books I write. As a teacher, it's my responsibility to advise people of the various pitfalls, because many spiritual seekers, you know, are enthused and very naive. And a lot of it sounds very glamorous, glamorous and entrancing. "I went to get a psychic reading, and he told me all about my grandmother's false teeth, and how could he have known? He must have known." I mean, you know, it's very impressive when you walk into it. And of course, there are some people who are very intuitive, and they do guess quite a few things right. However, they have been very wrong, I'll tell you, too. One time, a trans-medium said, "Your grandmother said you should eat more greens or you'll get arthritis."

You need to know the calibrated level of what's on the other side, and you need to know the calibrated level of what's on this side—the trans-medium and the source. There's a glamour and a trap in it all, in that the lower astral is—see, one of the benefits of being a human is that the human has the choice of returning to God. The lower astral, by having refused it, does not have the choice. So, the lower astral hates the human because the human has no glass ceiling, no topside, and is not condemned to the hells that they exist in. So, one thing a lower astral loves is to get a naive spiritual seeker, especially one who is making good progress, and get control over 'em and lead 'em astray. The delight is that of mischief. The devil, the little devils love to pull somebody off the pathway and watch them go and sit out in their car in the middle of the desert, waiting for the aliens to come and get you. I mean, good God. I mean, you know, it happens every day. So, the naive are pulled in. I had a teacher who said never trust anything unless it's in a body. In other words, unless you can *see* who you're talking to, or their writings, let's say, somebody who either does or has existed in human form, because you have no idea what you're dealing with.

And other universes are extremely complex, subtle, and ingenious. Spiritual deception is a long and honored tradition in India. They've been at it for thousands of years before you were even thought of. They were expert at it in those years, and they are expert in it today. It's a tradition. All kinds of manipulations of seemingly magical and wondrous events, huh. The spiritual seeker is best to stay with that which is safe, that which calibrates over 200. For instance, the *Course in Miracles* calibrates at 600, yeah? All right, 600 is a pretty pure pathway to follow. So, if you know the calibrated level of that which you're following, you avoid the lower astral. The lower astral hates That Which Is, you might say; hates love and hates divinity, and it seeks to subvert truth.

So, the lower-astral influences are what convinced Islamics to think that killing people for Allah will get them to heaven. I mean, that's an obvious, severe distortion; and yet, if you get people young enough and small enough and begin brainwashing them with this belief, they will believe it by the time they grow up. Nazi Germany did it with the German youth; they didn't know any different, didn't know any better. So, it seems to me that Revelations was a way in which the lower astral got into the New Testament, which was a huge threat to it. The New Testament, especially if you read the translation from the Aramaic rather than from the Greek, calibrates extremely high if you take out Revelations. Take out Revelations, it calibrates extremely high and it has extreme power. So, to sort of disable it to some degree, that which is its opposite was placed right in the middle. And you'll notice that the extreme right wing of Christianity plays off Revelations. You know, when it shakes its fist with hatred of the sinner and death and hellfire, that all plays out of the Revelations, out of Revelations.

So that particular wing of Christianity would feel threatened if you diminish the validity of Revelations, because their whole ministry is based on that. Well, it sounds very pious to hate sin, except that hatred is hatred, isn't it? To hate a bad man is the same as hating a good man. I mean, what holds you down is the hatred itself. So, to hate sin is really not a very cool place to be.

Anyway, the visions that John had—John himself calibrated at 70, just like the book of Revelation calibrates at 70. The vision that John had is a lower-astral reality. It was related to me by a very well-known teacher in Sedona who was in that place and saw what was going to happen. He gathered all his followers; they prepared for the end times, and all that. The end times had a great big play again with all the psychics. Everybody who got a reading heard about the end times and how New York was going to crack down 14th Street—there was a big fault under 14th Street, right under the best German restaurant in New York City, on 14th Street. California was going to fall off in the ocean, Phoenix was going to become a seaport. Remember all that? People were building underground houses and dome houses. So, that was a hysteria that spread, and so that kind of teaching . . .

How to tell that teaching right off the bat without calibrating it is simple. *That which comes from God brings peace, and anything that brings anything other than peace and love is not of God.* That *is* the rule of discernment. So, you don't have to calibrate everything, because perception as the third eye of the Buddhic Body opens up. One perceives that which is of God and that which is not of God, you see. And that which is not of God becomes an absurdity. But there're all kinds of people; they're still practicing in Sedona, by the way. I see their names—somebody gave me a list of their names off the Internet. So, the same creatures that were predicting California falling off in the ocean, and God knows what all. The little people coming to get us from other planets, and all. They're still practicing. They didn't go out. So, when the predicted end of the world came and the world didn't come to an end, they just changed the story. It's not going to be '87; it's going to be '93. Then '93 came and went.

So, lots of people have tuned in on that lower-astral thing—seeing the end of the world, the great apocalypse, and all. And on that astral level, it is a reality. On that level, it is a reality. "The level which was perceived by John is a reality, resist." (True.) "On the lower-astral level, resist." (True.) "It is a reality on this planet, resist." (Not true.) Sorry, wrong universe! Okay. It is the truth, but not for this planet, folks. We said this morning there are many dimensions, and what's true in one dimension—you see, there's movies going on in each dimension, and their movie is not our movie, what was seen by those people. Now, the person that told me that out here in Sedona was a well-known teacher and he literally believed it because he experienced it, and I'm sure John who gave us Revelations, it was a literal experience. All right.

There are many mental disorders due to a genetic problem. All mental disorders are due to brain chemistry, on the operational level. A third of the planet has an insufficiency of serotonin, not enough serotonin in their brain, that essential neurotransmitter to keep them out of depression addiction, gambling addiction. There's not enough serotonin, and they go into depression. Depression is the most prevalent and largest illness in the United States. One-third of the population is subject to depression. And I believe operationally, the best thing to do with it is like you wear glasses if you're nearsighted—you just take something that raises the serotonin, because you're making up for a genetic defect.

All right, I'm sure it has karmic antecedents as well. So, I tell people in the office, do what you can to raise the neurotransmitter and do what you can to evolve as far as you can spiritually. Also, we're not talking about karma today, but karmic research will almost always take you back to the lifetime that precipitated the depression in this lifetime—the penance that you're paying now for what you said or did in that lifetime. One can also go into the lower astral through psychic events, drugs, LSD—the so-called bad trip is nothing but a trip in the lower astral. Nightmares, hallucinations, imaginations. So, one can plunge unwittingly into the lower astral. Nightmares are probably one of the commonest ones.

One can have difficulty with other neurotransmitters in the brain. See, there is an infinite number of transmissions going on psychically, as well as electronically and otherwise, in an infinite multitude of universes. So, the brain wouldn't know what in the world to pick up. Yeah. When I was young, radio was new. Radio was a novelty, like the Internet is now. It was a novelty. And I remember we got a radio—in fact, we didn't have a radio, so I made one, a crystal radio. And we wound the coils ourself and did all that. We had a cat's whisker that you poked around until you got a station, oh, God. But you had to afford earphones, which I didn't have the money for earphones, so I'd have to buy earphones to live with this thing. But anyway, what your radio does, it has limiter circuits. The radio, you look at your station dial on the radio, the old-fashioned radio—AMs, you know—it has limiting circuits; otherwise, every time you turn your radio on, you're going to get about eight stations at once, eight stations coming in at once. So, these limiting circuits are to screen out other frequencies. Well, there are certain kinds of mental disorders where that neurotransmitter that energizes that system to keep out other frequencies is missing or deficient, or due to some life event, it gets diminished, and I'm sure there's some karmic propensity. And the people will literally experience one of the levels of hell. So, I always tell people if such a thing should occur to you, just presume that—just take my say-so—in some other lifetime you cursed somebody to hell, and that karma is coming back. And therefore, here's what I would do—if you get into a hellish state, start praying up a storm. Say, "Dear God, in that lifetime I did not realize what I was doing when I cursed somebody to hell and I ask for forgiveness, and I ask that person's forgiveness, and I forgive myself for that ignorance." And, because in a way, one can bring hell upon oneself by cursing another to hell, right? So, you simultaneously undo the karma the best you can. You try to undo whatever you might have done.

Whenever anything negative befalls you, it's always very practical to presume it's some kind of karma coming back! If you treat it as though it's some karma from some previous lifetime, you don't have to literally know it. Just guess that's likely so and do what you can to undo that via forgiveness, forgiving yourself, forgiving the other person.

Below level 600, it's not likely that a person's going to remember a past lifetime. I never asked that question, whether people actually remember their past lifetimes. Well, I guess they do. "People under 600 do remember past lifetimes, resist." (True.) Yeah. "Especially infants, resist." (True.) Especially children. Yeah, people do remember that. But, let's say something befalls you in this lifetime. You may not recall, you know, what went on in some lifetime. But you're on pretty good grounds to presume that that is the likelihood, and handle it as though that is what occurred, yeah.

Things occur because of such complex conditions. Now, we said that nothing causes anything else, so an event here, you might say, precipitates a climate, and that climate is what interacts with that which you are to precipitate a certain event. You understand that it's not *causing* it. It's a favorable condition in which that can come forth. Many things that you think is a calamity is something that actually, through your spiritual commitment, you brought back because of your wish to undo it. I went through surgery for a hernia without anesthesia. It was excruciating, and I remembered exactly what I'd done. I was reliving exactly what I'd done. In that war, you know, with a sword, I gored this guy through the groin—and that wasn't the error. He was down and out. The error was, I didn't finish him off. The guilt of that lasted to this lifetime. Out of true compassion, I would have finished it for him so he didn't have to die a slow, lingering death of infection and days and weeks of agonizing pain before he went, but I didn't. I lacked the moral courage to do the honest thing. In another lifetime I didn't make that mistake. He and I killed each other at the same time. I've told you about him. Yeah. Anyway.

So, the undoing, then, the forgiveness of that, the guilt of that brought back the opportunity to re-experience and to forgive myself, because the guilt of that to a warrior's conscience—not to another person's conscience, but to the consciousness of a warrior—that was a cowardly thing to do. And the cowardice of not killing him off lasted all those lifetimes. It wasn't that many lifetimes ago, but anyway. So, you just got me talking about karma here. Sorry, we started off on Revelation and ended up . . . I already told you about Mohammad and the Islam guy. He and I got into it during the Crusades and killed each other at the same time, you know. Yeah. I killed him for Jesus, and he killed me for Allah at the same time. We were good, and I got him right through the heart, and he killed me deader than a mackerel. And we went out of body and both started hysterical laughing. I did it for Jesus, and he said, "I did it for Allah." It just broke us up, you know. It was hysterical. We've been great pals for many a lifetime.

Q: *"What is the most direct path to the consciousness level 500?"*

Well, we did it this morning. The willingness to let go the payoffs of the ego, the gratifications, the feelings of justification, the willingness to feel victorious at another person's expense. What you have to remind yourself is, although what you're getting out of this ego position has a certain pleasure, it is not happiness. You get pleasure out of turning the knife in somebody's back, but you don't get happiness out of it. So, if you let go of the pleasure of revenge, let's say, what you get is the happiness of being a freer, more loving, and therefore self-loving spirit. So, there is an enormous payoff. You get back far more than you let go of.

Q: *"How can you avoid getting false answers in the kinesiology process?"*

I explained it before. It's your intention—you see, I would have to go back and explain the physics of kinesiology. The physics of kinesiology has to do with the fact that consciousness recognizes that which is, and it does not recognize that which is not. Therefore, that which is false, because it is not, gets no response. The intentions of the two people—when you do kinesiology, it's best to not care one way or the other about the answer. And you won't always get the answer that pleases you, or the answer that you think you'll get. The answer you get is irrespective of the test subject, and it's really irrespective of your own belief system. Because we've tested over many times, and I've done it on videotapes which many of you probably have at home, in which we test things out which are completely opposite of what everybody believes, and we still get the correct answer. And we've done it, you know, in front of large populations, and it's been done by thousands of practitioners for many years. One, I remember, it was done in Korea, in which we held up two apples and—no, there was two packages of cabbage, right. Somebody gave us a package of cabbage. I held it up, and we were all ones and twos, you know, made everybody go strong. Then we held up the other cabbage, and it made everybody go weak. I didn't know what it was. She said, "Well, this one's got pesticide, and this one doesn't." So, it's irrespective of your belief system. The best test subjects are children. And I think in *Power vs. Force, Volume I* video, we test organic tobacco versus commercial tobacco, and we test a picture of Hitler in a brown envelope, and all. We used a little child, and of course, the answers were all correct.

Q: *"How is discernment different than judgment?"*

Well, discernment, spiritual discernment, is the opening of the third eye. It's one of the gifts of the Spirit. And it has nothing to do with judgment. Discernment is noticing whether it's a rainy day or a sunny day, and it's not a moral, judgmental matter. Judgment is bringing in an additional dimension of ethics, morality, spiritual belief systems, et cetera. In dealing with the so-called New Age community and all of its attractions, it's a carnival, it has many attractions. Discernment is considerable. Usually, judgment is not involved, because many of these people who have all these various practices, you know, themselves believe in it. I mean, they're not out to con you, but because they themselves are part of the cadre that have been caught into the belief system themselves. There's, heh, one currently on the Internet about a local spiritual group, with a description of how this group operates. It was right out of the book I had written on how to recognize a cult. It was like right out of . . . yeah, and uh . . . and the leader of this group gets messages from the other side. He's got, uh, I don't know . . . they always call him Michael or Baba something or other. Anyway, here's this spirit on the other side. So this guy goes and writes up four fallacious statements and goes to this guy, who consults his spirit guide. His spirit guide gives him a reading on these four questions. All of them are fallacious—about the spirit of his four-year-old daughter. He never had a four-year-old daughter. One was about his first wife—he never was married before. All four were totally fallacious, and yet he got an elaborate reading on each and every one of them; you know what I'm saying?

Q: *"What are the names of the individuals that currently calibrate over 700?"*

I don't know any people over 700. I wouldn't know the names of them. What we've asked is, how many? See, we're trying to get the distribution of the levels of consciousness on the planet, how it plays out. So, we were asking that mainly to see how the levels play out. And I don't know who they would be. All I know is, there are approximate numbers, approximate numbers. But we can ask about it.

So, we asked how many people are there. It has changed, by the way. First of all, this change was, the number of people who calibrate over 200 since 1995 has shifted. The number of people below 200 is now only 78 percent. It was like 85 percent; 7 percent of the population since we first wrote the book has shifted from the negative to the positive range. The number of people over 600 has also increased. Let's see. I forgot what I wrote now. It probably changes. "Over 700, there are more than 50 people, resist." (Not true.) "There's more than 30 people, resist." (Not true.) "There's more than 20 people, resist." (True.) "21." (True.) "22." (True.) "23." (True.) "24." (True.) "25." (True.) "26." (True.) "27." (True.) "28." (True.) "29." (Not true.) All right. So, at this moment it says there are 29 people on the planet over 700.

In the sense of the silence, the silence—the sense of oneness is all one and the same thing. The silence, the Self, that which you are, all of existence is a totality of which there is no witness. The witness and that which is witnessed are one and the same. There is no "this" witnessing a "that." Because there is no "this" and "that"; there is only that which is. There would have to be a "this" witnessing a "that," which is not the way it works.

Q: "Do you recommend antidepressants?"

Yes, I think so. I don't see any point to suffer needlessly. And if you get out of the depression, then you can go back to establishing a life that is as supportive as you can. And depressions are periodic; they come on cyclically; they come on for many reasons unknown. Many of them are temporary. And some are biological; bipolar disorder, there's a genetic factor. So, because it's like diabetes for which you take insulin, or migraine headaches for which you take Imitrex, there's no point to lie on the bed all day with a migraine when there's now some medications that will cure it within an hour. There's no point to suffering. Because a person who's spiritually committed, all their intentions, because of the spiritual intention of the Spiritual Will, all that occurs can be made to serve one's spiritual intention. All suffering, all seeming misfortune has a coloration, an aspect, a significance if it's contextualized in a certain way. It can be made to serve one's spiritual purpose.

Q: "Can a person evolve up the scale of consciousness without experiencing the lower level of it?"

Well, I don't know. Can you be a human being without once having been a worm? I don't know. It isn't that the person so much evolves, it's that consciousness evolves. So, that consciousness at this level would choose this kind of animal, or body, or plant, or wherever that consciousness is at that time. We did an interesting thing. We'll confirm this also, for the fun of it. "The spirit, the human spirit enters the fetus before the first month, resist." (Not true.) "Before the second month, resist." (Not true.) "Before the third month, resist." (Not true.) "The human spirit enters the embryo after the third month, resist." (True.) The human spirit. So, the embryo is a potential home for the human spirit. But it's not until the third month that it actually chooses to energize and join with that embryo, huh. So, it could be that one more or less chooses an incarnation that's consistent with one's level of consciousness. Had the body been that of a worm there on the snowbank, I probably would not have gone back in it even if my father was there. It just wouldn't have been suitable, you know what I mean?

A mantra is a different meditation. We'll talk about meditation techniques later on in the courses. A mantra is a very specific thing. Many times, it's the teaching of a very specific school, in which the consciousness level of the school itself plays a part. The consciousness level of the teacher plays a part. We recently did one, we calibrated the level of—oh dear, a Sanskrit classic translated by, I think, Satchitananda. Yeah. All right. That certainly would sound legitimate, right? *Sutras of Patanjali.* "The mantra *Ohmm* calibrates over 500." (True.) "Ohhmmm, over 600." (True.) "Ohmmmm, over 700." "Ohhmmm, over 740." (Not true.) "Ohhmmmm, about 700." (True.) Ohmmm, about 700. All right. The way it was written in this translation from *The Sutras of Patanjali* was "Aum." "'Au-um' calibrates over 200, resist." (Not true.) So, whether you're going "aum" all day or you're going "ohm" all day means you go to heaven or hell, folks. I hate to tell you, you get the wrong book, it's curtains. All right. So, I would test out the level of the mantra. There are many mantras that make you go weak. Test out the level. See, you would say, well . . . See how you instantly get blinded? Well, *Sutras of Patanjali*: Amen, right? Translated by Satchitananda, amen! It's got to be the absolute truth.

The TM meditation, those of us who've done TM, we were given a private mantra. I never investigated it. "The TM mantra I was given is over 200, resist." (True.) Whew! "It was over 300, resist." (True.) "350." (True.) "390." (Not true.) Anyway, it was over 200, so . . .

You see, a thing doesn't have to calibrate at 800 to be worth studying, because things are not useful except at your own level. If you're worrying about how to forgive your mother-in-law, reading something by Krishna—you know, the Bhagavad Gita—is not going to help you much. Krishna says, "I am the Supreme Being, the Ultimate Reality of all." Does that help you with your mother-in-law? Not much. You might do a lot better to pick a spiritual program that calibrates around 300 and tells you how to get off personalizing other people's problems. You might do better going to an Al-Anon group or, um, you know, because . . . So, just a calibration doesn't mean anything except that it's pertinent to that level.

You know, I think I've told you in a previous lecture, when I was born into this body, I was three, the body was three. And suddenly, out of the Void, the nothingness of the Hinayana Voidness, which I believed was the ultimate truth from those lifetimes. Suddenly there was the stunning awareness of existence. Awareness of existence *as* existence. I was conscious that I existed. Instantly came the fear of nonexistence. Hmm. First of all, I wasn't happy to exist in the first place. To be in a body again was not a delight. To be alive as a human being was not a pleasure at all. I was not happy with existence; but even though I wasn't happy with existence as a physical human being, the fear of nonexistence then came up. Well, the duality of existence of the Self, the reality of the Self as existence versus nonexistence, is not a problem until you get to 840. "That's a problem that doesn't arise until about level 840." (True.) Yeah. It's not a problem until 840. So, you really don't have to study how to transcend existence versus nonexistence until you get there, any more than you need a map to Cincinnati when you're not even in Ohio yet.

So I think one should look: What are the kind of problems I'm having right now? And then, of course, most people in spiritual work are aware, you know—and have met and mingled with others. If you're having trouble forgiving your mother-in-law, then what you really need is the *Course in Miracles*, right? You don't need *The Sutras of Patanjali*. All spiritual work is beneficial because of the intention behind it. It's the intention that sets the calibrated level. So, when you seek out a spiritual practice, teaching group—and many of us as we evolve go through a number of groups. We've checked out Reiki, we've checked out the Boy Scouts, the *Course in Miracles*, all of them. We've checked them all out, and each one of them has had a value, but it's not designed to take you all the way to Enlightenment. However, you can't get to the top floor without walking the stairs, right? So, you can't get from the second floor to the fourth floor without going through the third floor. So, each spiritual practice and teaching has its own intrinsic value and beauty.

Spiritual Beauty and Bliss

Even though I became an atheist later on, as a child I was brought up High Episcopal. And it was in a cathedral, and it was gorgeous—stained-glass windows, incredible architecture. And later in life, when I tour Europe, I go from cathedral to cathedral. I go from Cologne to Reims—my interest in Europe is the cathedrals because it is the greatest creative work of man. It combines the incredible architecture, incredible beauty, incredible commitment and work, incredible frescoes and paintings, carvings. You can look at a carving that a man has spent his entire lifetime carving that pulpit. One entire lifetime. Everything in third and fourth dimension, and magnificent. And then of course, the incense over the couple of hundred years embeds itself in the wood. And then of course, you have the pageantry of the parade of the bishop and the miter and the incense. And I was the bishop's boat boy, and he would incense the parishioners. And I was the little guy with the long coat on and I held up the incense, and he would put it over the charcoal. So, those things were inspirational.

You might say it reinforces a love of beauty, and one part of spiritual practice, I think, is an increasing sensitivity to beauty. And certainly, by the time you get to the high 500s, the beauty is stunning. In fact, it is incapacitating. You can, of course, get incapacitated along the way. The high 500s is one place you can get incapacitated. As you get up around 580 or 590, the stunning beauty of the world makes you cry all the time. You can turn a corner, and the beauty of it just knocks you out and you're really not too functional in the world. And a lot of people come out to Sedona in that level. You know you just can't function in the world anymore. Or, a couple look at each other. You're in the airport and this couple look at each other, and you can see the love between them. Just the sight of that love just knocks you out. You're just overwhelmed. So, that's the level of the high 500s, which is approaching bliss. Your sensitivity to beauty. You can see beauty in everything.

And I say the easiest place to see beauty is the Kleenex box. You pull the Kleenex box half out, and you see it's like a painting by Georgia O'Keeffe. You really see the beauty of the Kleenex box; you see its incredible beauty. It stands there, you see, because you're beyond form now and what you're seeing is the intrinsic beauty and perfection of all of creation. Every Kleenex box is an opportunity to see God! That's the truth. And at the very high 500s, I can remember walking down alleys and I was just struck by the beauty of it. It was like an impressionistic painting. And the garbage can is all lumped over like that, and it's like a piece of sculpture, you see. All the world turns into beautiful sculpture. Everything you look at, you can see the perfection and the intrinsic beauty of existence. All that exists has an intrinsic, incredible beauty. The capacity to see it, then, is like a gift, a spiritual gift. As you go maybe around 560 or 570, the incredible beauty of everything knocks you out, and that makes it very hard to function in the world. It does.

And I remember in New York City, looking down—this what the world would call a disgusting, filthy alley, probably full of dead cats and rats and druggies, and it was just like an incredible French impressionistic painting. Everything stands there. There's a movie, *The Red Shoes* ballet, which was done many, many years ago. I think the Sadler's Wells ballet played in it, played the ballet. And in there, I think there's a street scene and the newspaper is blowing down the street, and as the wind blows it down this dusty street, you see this newspaper doing a dance all of its own. It was made in Europe. I don't know if it's available in the video stores, probably not. But the famous ballerina of the Sadler's Wells in those days played the lead part in the *Swan Lake* ballet, which was incredible. So, the increasing attraction of beauty, the ability to see beauty in all that exists is part of spiritual evolution, I think.

Q: "When you talk about the Holy Spirit, are you talking about what the Course in Miracles *talks about?"*

My understanding of it, yeah. Classically, God is described as being transcendent or immanent. The experience of God within is the pathway of Enlightenment. Religion is traditionally devoted to the experience of God transcendent, in which case God gets displaced in time. The traditional religionist believes that God set up the universe, and like a bunch of billiard balls, it's been running itself ever since. You live a lifetime and then you go to heaven. So, in the meantime—so, God started the universe, took off, and is waiting for you in heaven. Hopefully you've led a good life, which it will be a pleasant encounter. Otherwise, God help ya. The presence of God within is the province of the mystic, huh? The traditional religion is a very interesting paradox, because it is the presence of God within, it was the mystic that is the source of all the world's religions, who then claim that the only valid God is a transcendent one; other than Christianity, where Christ says that "Heaven is within you."

In the Muslim world, Mohammad calibrates at 700. And in the Muslim world, the enlightenment of the mystic is considered a heresy. It's considered to be a claim. Well, to the unenlightened person, such a statement seems like a claim, but the person to whom that's a reality, it has nothing to do with a claim—there is nothing to claim and no one claiming it, because it is ordinary reality. It's ordinary reality, yeah. Just as a big, strong man can pick up a hundred pounds like it's nothing—that's just normal to him; that's not an exceptional thing, that's not an accomplishment, that's not something that he looks to the world for acclaim for. It's just that he's born that way and he is that way, and he can pick up a hundred pounds like it's nothing. Who's that big, bald basketball player? Shaquille O'Neal. Anyway, he's 7 feet tall and he weighs 380 pounds, or something. He could probably just lift this table up like it's nothing, you know what I mean? My eyes would bulge. So, to a person whose eyes would bulge trying to lift this up, it would seem like an incredible accomplishment. To him it would be a snap, you understand? So, the reality of the mystic is only the way it *is* to the mystic; it is nothing particularly unusual or important. When it comes on, it knocks you out, when it starts. But after, as the years go by, you learn how to live with it. It's just ordinary.

The Holy Spirit then is the expression of God within as it becomes known. You might say, I look at the Holy Spirit as a connection between the infinite nonlinear and the linear. It's like the connection between the infinite nonlinear. What is the connection between form and non-form? Within all of form *is* non-form, yeah? We said that from a scientific viewpoint, the quantum potentiality is the space. Ah! There we got the Holy Spirit and the quantum potentiality. Wait until the Holy Spirit hears about this! "That's where it's at, resist." (True.) By God, that's where it's at. Just discovered it a few weeks ago—I was writing something; I said, "That's the quantum potentiality, man!" Where the infinite potentiality of the manifest contacts the manifest and influences it. I always think of the Holy Spirit as in that 1/10,000th of a second between two thoughts that the Buddha talked about. I remember when I first read that, that was so frustrating. I was really mad. I tried meditating and finding a 1/10th of a second between two thoughts, and you can't do it. It's like a dog chasing its tail. The harder you try to create a space between two thoughts, the more impossible it becomes. And yet the Buddha said that's where you glimpse eternity. And it is a fact; it is a fact. And in that instant, the Holy Spirit takes advantage of that space, and it leaps in with that knowingness. So, the presence of God as it expresses through the *purusha*, the Sanskrit word for the presence of—Purusha is . . . what would we say . . . ? People say, "When you're talking, what is it that's talking?" . . . because there is no personal self that's talking. The talkingness is happening of its own. There is no talker talking. There is no "this" doing a "that." The talkingness is complete and spontaneously happening of its own. In the spiritual teacher, that's classically in Sanskrit called the "purusha." The knowingness within the Self with a capital *S*, which speaks and is able to express is, to me, an aspect of what the *Course in Miracles* calls the Holy Spirit.

The awareness of spiritual truth comes about spontaneously as a knowingness. It doesn't come about as a progression of logical thought. It's a knowingness. You might say, as the small self dissolves into the larger Self, the larger Self, because it *is* all things, knows all things. So, a question, then, in the mind, like, finesses a response just as the kinesiologic test does. The knowingness is absolute and certain; therefore, the consciousness, the awareness, and the teaching of a mystic is completely different than a religionist's, because the religionist has obtained the information from elsewhere, from an authority somewhere in time. So, religion, then, comes from an authoritative base, in which the teacher of religion is not speaking from that which is within the teacher but what one has heard. Therefore, it's vulnerable; therefore, it has to be defended; therefore, it's presented in an authoritarian way.

The spiritual Reality is absolute. The certainty is absolute, and therefore no authority is necessary; nor is it arguable, nor does it make any difference whether anybody listens or believes it or not. It's completely inconsequential. So, one is in a different position than religion, in which authority has to be cited and you need a whole ecclesiastic structure with titles to warrant the authority, but the authority does not come from within. However, there are certainly excellent teachers who have not experienced the truth which they're teaching, but they are excellent teachers of that which they have heard about. So, as long as they say they quote the source of the teaching, they're authentic and they're integrous. If the source of what one is teaching is a certain doctrine and one quotes that as the doctrine, then that's integrous because that is the source of your teaching; and it may or may not be integrous; it may or may not be accurate—you don't know. You'd have to test it with kinesiology to confirm whether it's true. Within the spiritual experience of the Absolute, you don't—there's no need to test anything, because it is glaringly the Reality of one's existence and of that all around you; so every question then answers itself. It doesn't have to be defended, so it's not arguable. No one has to defend any doctrine, because there is no doctrine. There's only

That Which Is, which is absolutely, glaringly obvious. That which is absolutely glaringly obvious only needs acknowledgment of that which it is. You know what I'm saying? Anything else? We got off into a serious vein here. Those questions are just too serious!

Q: "If we are just witnessing and everything is happening of its own, what is the function of decisions and Spiritual Will making a decision? Is that just a top lifetime theme?"

We said that the karma is set by spiritual intention and commitment. Everything that happens in the universe, then, is set by that which it is. And when you affirm or make a certain decision, then you've, like, changed the charge on your little particle. And your fate in the universe will be different because you just changed the particle. When you come out of the pit, where in the pit of hell—whose agony is beyond any description, although Dante was pretty close—in the absolute pits of hell, when a voice comes up and says, "If there is a God, I ask him to help me," that changed the polarity of that particle. Instantly that particle, and infinite magnetic power of God, pulled that particle right into the space of infinite splendor, and the ego died. And one-tenth of a second before that, the entity was in hell. You say, "How can an entity in the pits of hell, despair and agony, and black, total despair, which went on forever, forever, then access a space that is indescribably magnificent?" Because first of all, there is no temporality to temporality. So, what seems to be sequential was only a perceptual—it was only a perceptual sequence. It didn't happen in Reality. Whew! But that was the seeming sequence, seeming sequence. So, to commit, then, from: "I am all there is, there is no God," to "I ask God to help me" is surrendering one's will. And as Ramana Maharshi says, "There's two ways to get to Enlightenment. One is to ask, 'Who am I?' and the other is to completely, totally surrender one's ego to God." One's will to God. So, that was the instant: surrendering the will to God at that instant. There was certainly no thought that the Self was Divinity immanent. That would seem like a very comical joke in hell!

Q: "Can you give an example of a spiritual intention, and how to go about having one?"

Let's say, if you grew up in the Midwest in the '30s like I did, if you hit your thumb with a hammer, your father would say, "Goddammit!" Your grandfather would also do that. I had one grandfather, when he got mad, he'd build up. He'd go a long time, and then he'd get mad. He'd just curse a blue streak, and it would just go on, you know.

Well, that impresses the psyche of the boy who identifies with the father figure. Later on in life, you hit your thumb with a hammer and you find yourself saying the same thing. Well, to use the name of God in vain is a violation of one of the 12 commandments. You are not supposed to do that. So, it's like an instant reflex. You're not really blaspheming in the way that "blaspheme" is meant. Blaspheming as blasphemy is a conscious decision—to will that or think that or say that. No, this is sort of a dumb reflex, but anyway, it brings up guilt every time it happens. And I'd have to go to confession. High Episcopal—every Saturday afternoon, you've got to go to confession just like Catholicism and tell the Father, "I have sinned." So, anyway, eventually your intention is to stop doing that. All right. So, your intention is, it's happening really against your spiritual will. So, you work on it and you work on it, and sometimes it takes years and years to get off that spontaneous expletive, because it is programmed so quickly and intensely when you're at an impressionable age and it's part of your whole identification with the macho maleness and father figures, and all . . .

So, the whole society goes with that identification. It's like smoking in World War II. I mean, to not smoke, you must be a wimp or really weird, you know. It's hard to get over it, because it's an identification with the whole generation, a whole ambiance, a whole lifestyle of World War II, the bonding of men to men. A guy gets his leg shot off, and as they bring him off and put him on the deck, he says, "Christ, let me have a cigarette." That's literally what the guy wants. Anybody got a Camel? Oh, God, a leg gone, and he wants a cigarette. It gave him a great relief. Why? Because he bonded with the courage of all of men everywhere who've suffered, that's all. You know, when I was going through that surgery—I've had other major surgeries which were totally painless, but this one was agonizing, the one in which I remember goring that poor son of a gun in the groin. And I identified with all the men on the battlefield in the Civil War. I pictured all the men laying there with their limbs torn off and without any narcotics. They're going through surgery, getting their legs sawed off by the surgeon. I said, "If they can do it, *I* can do it." Yeah? So, we gain great strength then.

My wife said when she went through childbirth, she thought of all the women through all time that'd done this, and therefore it's possible; and if it's possible, it gave her the courage to do it. So, we get that courage and that conviction from our identifications, and that comes out of our intention; that comes out of our intention to transcend our fear of pain and our capacity to experience out anything, even without anesthesia. And you come out of it with a new knowingness that you're capable of almost anything if you decide to do it. Resolution.

So, spiritual decision, then, is different. A spiritual decision is how you set the compass on the ship. You know, I was a mine-sweeper. So, when I was at the wheel, because I was a boatswain's mate—so, three degrees to starboard, three degrees to starboard; so you set it three degrees to starboard. But the ship is not always going to stay there. The prow is going up and down, and she yaws and she heaves. So, your intention is to bring her back on course. It doesn't mean that every wave put you off course. So, there is no point in excessive spiritual guilt and attacking yourself every time you use an expletive when you hit your thumb, because that's not your intention. So, your intention is what gets you to where you're going, and one degree off course makes a big difference. One degree off course, and after a couple of weeks at sea, you're going to end up on a different continent. Not only are you going to miss the port, you're going to miss the whole island. See, we said on the calibrated levels of consciousness, because they are logarithmic. These are logarithmic numbers. One degree, one point makes a big difference. One little change of spiritual intention makes a big difference.

So, even a minor decision like, "I wanna give up using the name of the Lord in vain"—so, I think the Lord is sensitive and will get upset by that? No. I consider God invincible, without positionality, without partiality; certainly not sensitive, vain, or anything else. For the good of the believer, one—it's for the good of the spiritual aspirant to revere Divinity. And therefore, to use the name of Divinity in vain diminishes one's own spiritual integrity. That's why it's not good. The naive person coming from ego translates it that God's gonna be offended and mad about that. I mean, why would—the Infinite Presence is like the sky; it's like infinite space. Would the sky take offense at a cloud? The sky is not affected by the cloud. The Infinite Divinity of God is beyond man's comprehension, and he keeps imagining that God is some kind of a superperson with a huge ego—a Divine ego, sensitive, paranoid, insecure, prone to rages and partiality. Also, this God of ancient times has favored geography and real estate, and favors people who live in this real estate or not that real estate; or promises them if they do this or that, this is your real estate. Now, can you tell me what an infinite Divinity—the Infinite Context out of which the whole universe arises—would have any special, heh, heh, favoritism as to who gets what real estate? God's not in the real estate business, is not sensitive, not paranoid, does not have a depressed serotonin level in his brain.

Even though that's a reality, there's nothing wrong with reverence for that which plays in our life as God, which, even if it is not identical with the reality of God as Krishna says, that the earned virtue is all the same. Even those who are devout in their pursuit of demigods or gods of, let's say, higher-astral realms who are not the Infinite Supreme, because of their devotion and surrender to me will be equally loved and favored, you know. The Bhagavad Gita calibrates at 900, so it's worth paying attention to. It's one of the highest spiritual ratings available.

CHAPTER 6

WITNESSING LEVELS OF CONSCIOUSNESS

Right now I am finishing the book called *I*, and then the book beyond that will have about a thousand calibrations, and many of the questions that were asked will be in that book. And many of them are frequent: "What about the Great White Brotherhood?" They calibrate about 700. "What about Alice Bailey?" She calibrates over 400. Many questions such as that. Somebody asked me about spirit guides. I've never really asked about spirit guides. "We have permission to ask about spirit guides." (True.) My feeling is that they're well-intentioned entities whose company you have earned through good karma from the celestial realms. "What I just said is true, resist." (True.) Okay. That's most likely what. That through some karmic merit one has the assistance of a, you might say, teacher. People call them spirit guides. I only had one such experience, I think. I went to the Monroe Institute and learned astral projection, and one time, in an altered state of consciousness—I think it was Level 12, for those of you who have done the Monroe tapes—I was concerned with something about the future, so I'm intentioning a vision about something off in the distant future. All of a sudden, a voice in my head said, "Try living one day at a time." Brought me back to reality.

The Monroe Institute was an interesting place. Monroe wrote *Journeys Out of the Body*, a very endearing book. Here's this naive engineer who'd never heard of out-of-body or any such things, and he starts astral projecting every night and having exciting adventures all over the astral universe, and some of them amorous. And then he comes back into the body in bed with his wife and he wakes up feeling guilty because he's had these adventures out there. And, Monroe, being an engineer, tried to use sound and the difference in frequencies between the two ears to set up an interval beat, and teach people how to go into an altered state of consciousness and go out of body in an altered state of consciousness. But I always thought Monroe was a very nice guy. He's now dead. You go there to Virginia for 10 days. You spend all day lying on a mattress, learning how to take off in various altered states. I remember one time I took off. Then we used to arrange to meet in various astral universes. One time I took off, and when I went back into the body, I went in upside down. Came back into the body. I went into the body and I'm looking at the back of my skull, down at the floor, and I had to back out of the body and redock.

The thymus thump, somebody asked me about. Taught by John Diamond, to activate the immune system. It's a useful way to quickly get out of a bad space. Breathe the energy up the spine to a higher chakra and do the thymus thump. At the same time, ask God for a miracle. If you're full of hatred, you've got too much energy in the spleen, so you picture the energy flowing up the tract—your spine up to the heart to love one's enemies, up to the throat to speak the truth, up to the third eye to see the truth, and up to God: that you surrender all such to Almighty God, et cetera. And do the thymus thump at the same time, and it works very good—and if you drink Diet Pepsi simultaneously, you can't go . . . Those are just quick emergencies when you're in a bad space.

Questions and Answers

Q: *"Is it a good idea to use the Map of Consciousness° to determine what level you are at?"*

Well, the purpose of the Map of Consciousness is to give you some kind of a general map. Energies tend to congregate, you might say—no, not "congregate"—let's say, "prevail"; tend to prevail.

We know there is such a thing as entrainment. So, if you subscribe to something, then to some degree you entrain with that level of consciousness on a nonlinear domain, and it has a certain dominance into your thought stream so that you tend to focus in, listen in. If the etheric is full of zillions of billions of possible thoughts and streams of thoughts, et cetera, why do you pick the one that you pick? Because you're probably tuned to a certain stratum. That's the danger of the MTV kind of entertainment; the danger of certain kinds of modern music. It began, I think, with heavy metal rock. I came out of the Motown sound, actually. It's a specific beat which John Diamond wrote about in *Your Body Doesn't Lie*. It's a so-called "anapestic" beat. The anapestic beat which is aligned with the music makes you go weak with kinesiology. So that if your hearing is blocked off with white sound and earmuffs and somebody plays that kind of music, you'll instantly go weak, and you'll stay weak for at least 20 minutes afterward. So, the entrainment of the consciousness of young people who put on headphones, they're entraining their consciousness—not to just the lyrics of the music—because the naive person thinks it is the lyrics of the music that's bad. No, that isn't bad, that's the good part. The bad part is the silent frequency vibration, the carrier wave. So, all these, you might say, are running on carrier waves. You pick up the carrier wave of that to which you ascribe.

There's a whole generation whose frequencies of the consciousness dominating their thinkingness is drawn from the lower astral. And they'll tell ya, "Why did you shoot your classmates?" "I don't know, I just wanted to see what it was like to kill somebody." I mean, is that bizarre, or what? Huh? Did that come out of this kid's mind? No, it came out of a field. That's the field that's dominating his consciousness. So, when you add drugs to it, which increases susceptibility, then you add an energy field which entrains the brain waves, and then you have him play a video game where you rip somebody else's heart out or kill them or mutilate them, and you have him do this 50, 100,000 times, so he's now a trained, brutal, heartless killer. That's what he is. He may look to you like a 12-year-old, but I see what he is. He's not a 12-year-old. He's already pulled a trained killer out of the astral which is occupying his consciousness right now. So, when he goes out and kills six or eight people with no feeling whatsoever, everybody thinks a 12-year-old did that. No 12-year-old did that. There was no 12-year-old there. The 12-year-old there left a long time ago, and he's now possessed by an entity that calibrates at that energy field. So, a whole generation of youth is being brainwashed, entrained, conditioned to do that which is thoughtless and uncaring. And the video games, there's a new one born every day. There is a new one called Riot, I think, or something. It's being produced in Hawaii or someplace, or China. Anyway, the whole game is to become part of a riot and destroy the city and destroy the town and kill the people, see. Now, the game is to do that over and over again. Well, how many times can you repetitively do a thing before it becomes second nature, huh? Like riding a bicycle; I mean, sooner or later, it's second nature.

Q: "Can you use the Map of Consciousness° to measure the level of growth in a person?"

No, that isn't really what it is for. It's more like a temperature scale. It is more like how the weather is there. It's more. You can tell by your prevailing level of commitment, by your prevailing view of God, yourself, the world, the process you're going through, your predominant emotional field. Most people can pretty much guess, you know, where you are. That's only of academic interest, anyway. It's a shorthand way of denoting a way of being in the world. Because each level has its lessons to be learned. Each level has its own gratifications. To commit to a manual project and complete it is very, very gratifying.

So, whatever the level you're at, it has its own challenges. Your challenge might be to forgive your mother-in-law and love her, no matter what, even if she is a "you-know-what." Well, the shift there, of course, is to shift your perception of her and your experience of her. Your spiritual commitment is the willingness to see her differently and forgiveness, and to stop personalizing it and see she's that way because that's the way she is. Not because of *you*, she's that way; it's because she's that way.

It's difficult to stop personalizing everything and putting yourself into the arena of everything that occurs in this world. People were that way before you were born. And they're going to be that way after you're dead, so there's no point in taking it personally! They're not doing it for your entertainment. They're doing it because that's the way they are. They're mean and gruff and nasty or self-centered, or whatever you wanna think they are, but they're not doing that 'cause of you; they're just doing that because that's the way they are, you know? So, to quit taking things personally means to become detached. That allows your perception of the person to be corrected. All of a sudden, it dawns on you that they're not being that way with *you*; they're just being that way because that's who they are. They're that way with themselves. And you stop feeling hurt because they're that way. Some people are gruff and mean and horrid. And they don't mean anything by it. They are just gruff, mean, and horrid.

There's where I go to the Girls Ranch. There is no doctor around, so I started going to the Girls Ranch. I've got 50 girls. And one nurse says to the other, "Don't pay any attention to him, he's just in grumping today." She's just affirming the reality, you know what I'm saying? I get there and I've got to make out all these forms that the government requires. "He's going to grump about the government." Sure enough, he did: "Goddamn government's always thinking of this—this is where all the taxpayers' money goes! And it's all useless and got nothing to do with getting this patient better, anyway. It's just bureaucratic baloney, you know." So, he's just grumping. That's all. He's not grumping at you. I wasn't grumping at the nurse. I didn't even know she was there. No, it's just, uh . . . See, that part of the personality which gets re-energized in order to maintain in the world is comical, and it just does whatever it does in response to the situation. But it's not yourself in the first place. And you can disconnect from it and discontinue it anytime you want. It runs on because society expects certain things, certain responses. At first you don't make any responses, and you withdraw from the world because there is nothing to say, nor is anyone really intelligible. It doesn't make any sense at all what people were saying, but after a while you learn how to be in the world, and it's entertaining. You don't take any of these rules personally. They're all just social roles that pop into the space because people expect you to say something. To make them happy, say something, you know what I mean?

Q: *"How can children be talked out of the video games?"*

It's a phenomena. It's like a porthole through which the lower astral pours into this domain. The most open porthole for the lower astral to this domain is the electronic media—MTV, the music that goes with that lifestyle; the languaging of it. The invalidation of the dignity of human life is subtle. Most adults are concerned about the lyrics, but it's not really the lyrics, although they probably play a small part. But "kill your sister," you're not going to start going around killing her because of that. But if your brain waves become entrained by a lower astral, you might just suddenly do it because you felt like doing it, because you wanted to see what it felt like to kill your sister. So, the motivation is different than what people think. They think it comes from the languaging. It doesn't. It comes from suggestion brought up by that energy field. "What I just said is a fact, resist." (True.) That's a fact. It isn't the lyrics, and it isn't the specifics. It is the unseen, invisible . . .

For the same reason, any spiritual teacher or teaching that you read, you are picking up a frequency and a vibration. And if you like Nisargadatta Maharaj, then you're probably going to like Ramana Maharshi as well, because they are both about 700. And the White Brotherhood is probably also going to make sense to you. So, if you're entrained to hear on that level, then you'll hear most things that are on that level. They will make sense to you, it will appeal to you. So, the teachers that appeal to you at different levels are appropriate for that particular level. Also, within yourself there's multiple personalities, you might say—multiple aspects to your personality, subpersonalities, archetypes, whatever you want to call them. And part of you may be attuned to one teacher and a part of you attuned to another. This one you really get a lot out of, and this one you don't, because you have different aspects to your personality, which is another thing that puzzles people in their spiritual work. One aspect of your life is going well, and another suddenly goes haywire.

Well, when you're single, you picture: "Oh, won't it be nice—the little, white picket fence and the little wife. Oh, golly, it's going to be so swell, and the little kids," you know. And then you get married and settle down, and all that. And now the duff that comes up wanting domestic bliss and happiness and security is satisfied. That goes down. The next step comes up: What about the wild, wonderful time all the singles are having out there? God, he can't wait to get out now and hit the road and meet with all the bimbos and the wild music and all the crazy strippers and, oh boy, oh boy, bikinis—they're wearing them downtown, and all. And he sees all this lurid stuff on television; he thinks, man, look what I'm missing! Locked up here with the wife and kids—the ball and chain. So he starts flirting with a girl at work, gets involved. They have a big fight over it. He leaves. Okay, now he's got his freedom. Wow! He's out there. He does you-know-what until he's blue in the face, until he can't do it anymore. After 12 or 13 different encounters, it suddenly gets raggedy again: "Jesus Christ, here I am all by myself with a bottle of whiskey, and she's left and I've got a hangover. I just hope she's not pregnant, and Christ, that cost me a fortune already!" He starts hankering for the little picket fence and the good wife and the kids. You see what I'm saying?

So, he quits his job, because now the adventurer wants to meet with danger, and he buys a race car, and he goes out there and drives like a crazy 20-year-old. And facing danger every day is what he's all about. So, you see how you shift from one thing—the next thing is his Harley. He jumps on his Harley. But the Harley driver, the wild, drunken Harley person now longs for the comfort of a family and a home. Right?

A funny thing, you know, you read these things, like in the paper *The Arizona Republic* a few weeks ago. There's always some guy cleaning his gun at home that shoots somebody in the family. It's amazing. He often shoots his wife or . . . A month ago, he shot his three-month-old. Now, imagine this guy. First of all, you've got to clean your gun in the presence of a family member, which, you know, is a severe violation of any kind of sanity. Not only that, but the gun is loaded, plus he's got the safety off the gun. Plus, all the objects in the room, this little-bitty thing about this big, and it's always a fatal shot. Never blows off their ear or blows off the toes of a three-year-old. No, it's always a fatal shot, instant death. How does he manage to forget the safety on the trigger, pointed exactly at the kid's heart? It's only a kid three months old, killed deader than a mackerel. Tell me how that happens, huh? He only was cleaning his gun with the safety off, and it just happened to be loaded with a bullet in it. And it just happened—when you think of all the points in the room it could have hit, it just happened to hit the three-month-old right smack in the heart. How does that happen? That was an actual case about a month ago.

You never read of a guy shooting his Harley-Davidson. "Man, I'm cleaning my gun and blew my Harley-Davidson right through the wall, yep." They never scratch their Harley-Davidson. They just kill the kids, the mother, the wife, the mother-in-law. Killed his grandmother while cleaning a gun. Those things make you think, huh?

Q: *"This morning you said, what we hold in mind comes into our life? So, if a lot of problems or difficult situations come into our lives, can we just change our intention and then get more different things?"*

It's just a metaphysical observation over the years, and rather common to many, that what you hold in mind tends to manifest. We were surmising that it could be that it operates via the quantum potentiality, the infinite quantum potentiality; that what you hold in mind, the energy of it literally affects the tendencies, the propensities, the likelihoods within the physical domain. You see, because the quantum potentiality is a potentiality, a potentiality, an infinite potentiality—not necessarily an actuality, but it is a potentiality. So, in the physics and mathematics of the nonlinear domain, so-called "chaos theory," the likelihood of "this" happening, you see, is a function of a nonlinear mathematical—we would think within the world of form—probability, but as you see from the Heisenberg principle, then a choice is going to perhaps increase the frequency with which "this" choice, "this" actuality manifests. Does that make any sense? It would be like you're increasing the charge on it. Anybody who's into spiritual work and tends to hold things—you see, and it has to be nonvolitional—it isn't like you say, "Dear God, I must have a new Mercedes Benz." You see? It's more like your love for it . . .

There's a certain car that I have loved all my life. And I don't have to have that car, haven't asked God for that car, but it's a beautiful car. A '46 Lincoln Continental, to me, was the most beautiful car ever made. It was elegant, it was beautifully proportioned. Great car. Anyway, a very rich man used to pick me up hitchhiking every morning in one. And I just loved that car, you see? So, all these years, every once in a while, I see something that reminds me of a '46 Lincoln. I've never seen one since on the road, but if one manifested, I wouldn't be surprised. So, it's more like you appreciate it, or you appreciate its special beauty, let's say, might tend to make it manifest.

Well, the places I've found to live over the years have always been exactly what I was holding in mind. Suddenly, somebody would call up and say, "The place right next to me is suddenly vacant, and you're the only one I want liven' there." So I said, "Okay." I went over there and looked at it, and by God, it was a little house out in the woods, right near the water. That's just what I had in mind. The same thing happened back east. I thought of a place in the middle of the woods. Sure enough, it suddenly came out of nowhere. It isn't that you're *causing* it; it's not that you're causing it, but from statistical probability, the mathematics of chaos theory, the likelihood is increasing as a result of your observation. You know that's the Heisenberg principle—that just merely thinking about it or observing it already changes the expected frequency of a certain occurrence, but it's done so nonmathematically. It's not within the capacity of differential calculus to say that. It is a non-statistical—we call it miraculous, huh? The miracle—we say in the *Course in Miracles,* if you ask the Holy Spirit for a miracle, you're already increasing the likelihood of that happening by the mere mentioning of it; the mere mentioning of it. So, the Heisenberg principle, which is the crossover, you might say, from the world of logic to the world of nonlinear, nonlogical, then, is to merely observe it, to merely think it already has changed the probability. You haven't *caused* it, but you've increased the probability.

What would Albert Einstein, Deepak Chopra calibrate on the Map of Consciousness®, and Mahatma Gandhi? Mahatma Gandhi is 700. Einstein was 499. Deepak Chopra, I don't know.

You see, the level of consciousness is set up by a great many things. One is karma; the other is spiritual intention, the degree of devotion, the willingness to surrender the benefits of the ego to the unknown benefits of the spirit—which are, unless you experience them, more of a hope than a reality. And you're taking it on faith from the word of others that surrendering these ego payoffs is worth the surrender. You don't really know yourself experientially that that's so. You know, it's like telling somebody, "If you give up addictive alcohol drinking, your life will be better." Well, he doesn't know that that's so. He can only take somebody else's word for it, but he doesn't really know, because he has no experience upon which to base that. So, the level of consciousness, then, is really a manifestation of your degree of commitment and your integrity and the level of the evolution of consciousness that you've reached.

People can make great jumps in one lifetime. When we said the statistical average for mankind as a whole is five points in a lifetime, many people go down. There are as many go down as go up, and some very extremely well-known people have gone down. If you calibrate their level of consciousness early in their career when they were at their peak, it's quite high. When you calibrate it later, they went down. Apparently, power over others, greed, the desire for whatever—followers, for control of others, fame or fortune; or the seduction of others, control of other people's minds. For some reason they fell and their level later in life is much lower.

That happened with Napoleon Bonaparte, for one thing. I think with Adolph Hitler, when he wrote *Mein Kampf*, his consciousness was considerably higher than it was a few years before his death.

And the same happened with Napoleon. Earlier in his career, he was an integrous military person, but then victory brought him megalomania. Rather than being grateful for his winnings, or satisfied by them, it created an egotistical cravingness. Let's ask if we have permission to do Napoleon. We'll just do Napoleon as an example. Napoleon at the height of his career: "We have permission to ask about Napoleon." (True.) "Was over 450." (True.) "460." (Not true.) Yeah, Napoleon was a very bright guy, and he calibrated a level of about 460. That is the level of presidents of the United States; they run around 450. Supreme Court justices run in the high 400s. Okay. "Napoleon, before he died, was over 200, resist." (Not true.) He went below 200 before he died. "He was over 70." (True.) "80." (True.) "85." (Not true.) So, from 450, he dove down to 85. So, whereas one can evolve spiritually, one can also succumb, and it's a matter of one's choices. You can see how success then becomes its own—the danger of success, which of course, is well-known. Success precedes—pride precedes a fall. So, to begin to believe your own publicity can lead to one's own downfall. So, Napoleon started out, you might say, as a legitimate military careerist, also became a very brilliant politician. And then succumbed to vanity and egotism and went down the tubes.

Q: *"Doctor Hawkins, when one such as Napoleon has made this drop in the level of consciousness, does the spirit gravitate toward that lower energy attractor pattern?"*

I don't know, because that would be a choice you would make. You're talking about the karmic propensity as he leaves the body at 70, or whatever he was at? That would bring us to the infinite justice of Creation. As we said that the infinite context out of which all of Creation arises one karmic unity. All that happens within the universe is happening spontaneously of its own, as a consequence of that which it is. That which it is. The operational reality of that which it is, is set up by its own intention, its own spiritual commitment. As you pray with great intensity and are willing to let go of the satisfaction of some ego benefit for a higher one, your polarity changes. The charge—if you picture yourself as a little iron filing, your polarity just changed, and so did the energy. The charge on your little particle just changed, right? The so-called "soul," that part which is nonphysical that leaves the physical body and determines one's karmic destiny, you might say is like a tiny computer chip. Within it is recorded all that's ever happened, every decision ever made; and all of that, you might say, accumulates as a certain weight and a certain polarity, even within the nonlinear domain, as though it had a design to it, so that it would fit "here" but not fit "there," be attracted to "this" but not attracted to "that."

So, in a giant electromagnetic field, when you turn on the power, everything within that field instantly lines up according to the power of the field. If you change the power of the field, everything in it instantly changes. So, if you're a little iron filing and you say yes to God, instantly you're pulled in this upward direction, and if you say no to God, instantly you are pulled in this downward direction, because your polarity is opposite. So, I always think of the lower astral as people whose polarity is the opposite of God; so, is repelled. So, you see people within your own lifetime who are actually repelled by love.

There's whole countries where love is illegal. You can be executed for exhibiting love, by Pol Pot's government. Any public exhibition of affection or love was punishable by instant death; actually illegal in the entire country. In Cambodia, any public display of affection or lovingness, and you could be put away or killed.

Q: "Recommendations on increasing serotonin, natural versus medication?"

I've tried them all, and many people who don't want to take medication, I'd say: why don't you try, you know, whatever was ostensibly helping depression at the time. I never saw any benefit from it.

It could be because in a doctor's office, you're not seeing the mild cases. You know, the mild cases that are amenable to naturopathic remedies, I probably didn't see, because it worked for them and therefore, they never saw me. So, what I probably saw was those cases more severe, where those particular remedies didn't work.

Q: *"I've heard that some people pray to Jesus, and some people pray to God. Does it make any difference?"*

I think the intention is different, or the intention can be the same. If the intention is the same, it doesn't really make any difference. I don't think it makes any difference, but we'll see. Well, in a way when you're praying to Jesus, you are asking for salvation. I mean, if you're praying to the aspect of Jesus Christ as Savior, that is one thing, right? If you are praying to Jesus Christ as God manifest, then that's a somewhat different motivation. "It makes no difference in which context one prays to Jesus Christ, resist." (Not true.) It does make a difference, hmm. "To pray to Jesus as Savior is different than praying to Jesus as God manifest, resist." (True.) "If we just pray to Jesus the same as if we were praying to God, the effect is the same, resist." (True.) Yes, because most people identify Jesus as God made man, so they're really praying to God. "Most people are praying to God made man, resist." (True.)

What would be the difference? When you're asking God for salvation, it's different than asking for enlightenment; the intention would be whether the intention is one of praise, acknowledgment, appeal. "So, the difference would be one in the intention, resist." (True.) "The intention of asking Jesus to be one's Savior is greater than praying to Jesus as God as acknowledgment, resist." (Not true.) "So, the acknowledgment of Jesus as God manifest is the highest intention, resist." (True.)

The inference that we get is, the intention is somewhat different. To acknowledge God manifest as man, as Jesus, and then to see Jesus as Savior is somewhat different. There's a subtlety. I don't know that in practicality it makes all that much difference. Let's see: "From a practical viewpoint, it doesn't make much difference, resist." (True.) That's what I suspected. That's what Krishna says: "No matter what name you might use for me, if your intention is devotional, if your devotion is to me as the Supreme, I will acknowledge you by whatever name you call me." Yeah. That's what Krishna says.

Q: *"You said earlier that we have a downside to our personality. And I'm wondering, do each of these aspects have their own calibration level, and is our calibratable level an average?"*

Yes. You see, all we've done is just, like, found a telescope and discovered that you can see the planets with it. And I mean, our knowledge of this is so rudimentary. It would take a large-size class in which we all divide up various projects and go into groups of three or four, and each one researches a project. All right. So, there's the various archetypes and subpersonalities. All of these have chakras. Right? All of them have chakras, and all of them have a karmic Anlage out of which they arose. You could be more familiar with one aspect of your personality and its history than others. Each level, each aspect, subpersonality then may have a different karmic source, a different calibrated level of consciousness. It could have a great deal of heart to it. It could have a great deal of solar plexus to it. It could have a great deal of wisdom to it. So, each aspect, then, of your personality could have its own evolutionary destiny and degree of wisdom and evolution. Some aspects of our personality may be quite perfected and others not so perfected. Certainly, the very fact that we are genderized in an animal body shows either a selection or a propensity or a karmic choice.

One could, after many lifetimes as a warrior, and a good one—I got everything you could get out of being the warrior. Can't go anymore with it. Choose not to be a warrior anymore. This lifetime—yeah, I was a warrior during World War II—but not really in the vein of a warrior. I was more in the—because there was no fear of death anymore, I served a totally different function than in any previous lifetime. But that pretty much finished off warrior, you know. Warrior's pretty much gone with me. But you could decide that your capacity to be affectionate to children and family-ness is what's lacking now in your personality and come back as a woman next time, to try to perfect those qualities more tradition- ally accepted as woman—the caringness for others. So, a person might make choices to balance out. However, that would not hap- pen once you reach a certain degree of enlightenment, because you're still working within form. What you're saying is, you want to perfect form; but once you transcend form, there's no point to perfect it. If I'm neither a warrior nor a mother, I don't have to per- fect either one, because that is not what I am, you know.

To realize the truth of that which you are would really be the ultimate destination and purpose for all of those selections. To feel oneself complete, to own one's muse and pursue music or art; to own the workman; to own the thinker, the student, you see. You can own all these various roles within yourself as though to perfect the personality, but if you're not the personality, there is no point to perfect it.

Q: *"At one point in enlightenment, there's no form, there's no body. Is that true?"*

The body is there as the same as anything else in the room. What changes is not your—it is not you, your self. On another level, it belongs to you. Not really "belongs" in the sense of possession; it's more like your shadow that follows you around. Your shad- ow belongs to you, and yet you're not your shadow. It seems that they're varied at various times, including disappearing as expe- riential reality. I think I described one time when I had left the world for some time and lived alone in really an ashram, a mon- astery for one person. That was me. And I'd forget to eat for peri- ods of time, and so on. I had a piece of cheese and a Diet Pepsi in the refrigerator; that was it. And I remember suddenly seeing this form in the mirror one day and I went into shock—"What in the world is that?" I thought it was somebody in the house with me. I laughed; I realized it was this body here. I went back and looked at it. Another time I walked through the wall, and that really hurt.

Walked smack into the wall. Just expected to walk right through it and was quite amazed that the wall and this physicality interfaced with stunning, uh—so there's identification with the body as though it's not even there. There's the lack of awareness of the body. There's a diminished interest in the body, so all these various aspects have happened. It's an entertaining, a puppet kind of accompaniment. It's more—I'd say at the present time, it's like a pet. It's a fun thing. I mean, I enjoy it. I enjoy it at times. But, I mean, it is a fun thing, and, um, especially if you get help taking care of it so it's not so much of a problem. You don't identify with it, that's all.

You see, these are not things you can really explain. But suddenly there's a shift where All That Is, one becomes the context. One is the context. One realizes one is the context, including all of the content. It's not excluding content. Because All That Is, the Oneness of All That Is, is not only context, but content as well. So, the body is within the content, but it's contextualized totally differently. Its appearance or its disappearance is of significance to other people. To oneself, it's of no significance. Whether it is or it isn't, comes or goes, is of really no significance. But it is of significance to others in the world, so it goes about its destined business. And I always call it a karmic windup toy. It just goes about its thing, whatever it's doing. It's talking here today, and without a body, you couldn't talk to people.

You ever try that? Having a conversation . . . so, it serves a purpose, and it runs its purposeful course which I think is sort of a . . . to me, I sense it like a karmic momentum. Like it's some kind of an agreement, and it was set upon its course.

You see a great ship at sea, a great oil tanker; when you shut off its engine, it doesn't stop. Its momentum, its propensity, it may take it five or six miles before it finally comes to a stop. So, I always have a feeling about the actions of this lifetime, that they're like a karmic, um, whatever, and that it just floats, it continues on its way through the water of its own. It's not paddling. It doesn't wish to go this way or that way. It just automatically floats that way.

We haven't talked today about love, you see. And we're saving that for another time. Huh!

We're trying to clear the decks for love. We're trying to remove all the positionalities of the ego, out of which come the dualities, which finesse the negativities which block love, want all the decks cleared before we even talk about love. So we haven't talked at all about the coloration, the change, the shift of perception and subjective awarenesses which come about as the heart chakra opens and the kundalini energy swamps you.

It's better not to be driving 75 on the highway when it happens, you know. It's better to slowly take your foot off the pedal. Do not put your brake on.

I see visitors from all over the world, and the diversity of spiritual experience is really amazing. An immense diversity of ways in which people experience the presence of Spirit within them, the different expressions. Some people will go into incredible states, but only under very specific conditions, conditions that are not even logical. They just don't go into a bliss state in the great cathedral; they go into it only in a purple elevator when it hits the 18th floor or something—very specific things: "I don't know, when I go into that elevator, I feel the presence of God, and when I'm not, I just don't feel it. I don't know." Almost as specific as that. Only very specific conditions or situations. In other people, it comes on spontaneously, unexpectedly, no warning. Right in the midst of the most unlikely activity comes an infinite Presence out of nowhere—unbidden, unasked, unexpected. So, the diversity of spiritual experience and how it is experienced; how it's experienced within the physical body—you were asking me about the physical body.

The spiritual work can bring on a great variety of experiences within the physical body. As you feel the energies begin to shift, you can feel very strange and bizarre sensations and vibrations going through your energy system—the peripheral energy system. You can feel incredible energies going up your spine and up your back, up into your brain, and very exquisite too. And then it pours down and goes out the heart and goes various places in the world unbidden and does mysterious things, all on its own.

Then there's levels of consciousness where the slightest imperfection in some aspect of some archetype from some time and place can bring, until it's cleared, a very painful sensation. Up to the 600s and 700s, it's extremely pleasant. Beyond that, it can become increasingly painful; periods of excruciating burning sensations. I was very happy to run across the fact that the Buddha said that. The Buddha said he felt like his bones were cracked, and he was attacked by demons and all kinds of things. So, it's like one pulls up, you might say, the impurities which are now extremely painful. In a lower energy field, you can dislike somebody and feel justified; in fact, even happy about it. As one's consciousness evolves, no such imperfection is allowed to pass. One may feel a sudden pain in the heart. You realize that the lady you didn't like on the streetcar is an imperfection, and what about her? Or you don't like people that look like so-and-so. For what reason? And then the memories come up and the forgiveness comes up, and then the pain disappears. So, there's also a level where any imperfection is absolutely, painfully intolerable. So, there's a great many different physical kinds of experiences that one can experience.

Those spiritual systems which rely on this pay a great deal of attention to the energy fields, the chakra systems, and the energy in the various chakra systems—the so-called "kundalini energy," are following a different emphasis, emphasis. But in the end, the same spiritual goals have to be accomplished. Whether you pull energy up from your toes to your heart or whether you learn to love your mother-in-law, it's all going to be the same; they both are going to have to be handled. But as you learn to love, the energy pours up of its own. I've never really checked out whether to what avail trying to manipulate the energies themselves, what they're good for. There's that very interesting book by Gopi Krishna called *Kundalini Energy*—I think that's the name of the book in which Gopi—remember, in that, he's meditating and he purposely is breathing energy up the spine to the crown chakra. All of a sudden, he feels a shot of exquisite energy, but it only hits one side of his brain. And after that, he's lopsided, totally lopsided. One side of him behaves in one way and the other side is the other way. You know, it's a very funny, interesting book, and very appealing, you know. So, I don't know. I think I would want a teacher pretty well advanced in manipulating energies for their own sake. I haven't researched that myself. There are certain specific practices which I have mentioned which can be handy.

Whether you can reach enlightenment by just sitting there in a meditative position and picturing light and energy going up to the crown chakra or not, I don't know. "Such is possibly the case, resist." (True.) Such is possibly the case "it would be fired by one's spiritual commitment, resist." (True.) Oh, the intention. The intensity of intention is already such a profound surrender to the Will of God that the mechanics of it, then, are only the out-picturing of that which has already been an inner spiritual decision, you know.

Let Go of Resisting the Sensation

It's funny, because when I lived like in a monastery, that was sort of what my life was. It was just one spiritual practice after another. Life was prayer and spiritual practice and meditation, and meditating for six to eight hours at a time, and not eating for days and becoming detached from everything in the world. If you felt the desire to eat, you instantly let go of the desire to eat. And you didn't eat unless you had no desire to eat.

Change the Pavlovian Conditioning

I later did a videotape on that, on how to lose weight. It's simple: never eat when you're hungry. See, because that is a conditioned reflex. You know, like Pavlov's bell. You feel hunger—first of all, you call that hunger—well, that empowers it already as hunger. The way to get over that is, never call it anything; never label anything. And that's how you can fall down and twist your ankle, and by surrendering to it, within minutes get up and walk away like nothing happened. You don't call it a twisted ankle. You don't call it pain. There's a nonverbal experiencing of whatever is flowing in toward you, and you let go resisting it completely and become one with it. As you do that, the pain leaves your ankle, and it becomes diffuse; you can feel the pain in your whole aura. And you completely and totally surrender to it, and you can't call it pain. If you call it pain, you're gonna suffer. You call it nothing at all. You just surrender to the presence of whatever that is, and within minutes it disappears, and you get up and you walk away. And that's how you take off weight. You can't call it hunger; that's labeling it and giving it power that it doesn't have. Instead, there's this sensation. What you do is, you lay down and you let go resisting the sensation, just like you do with the twisted ankle. Don't call it hunger; that's a program. You lay down and you let go resisting the sensation. You let go resisting the sensation. All of a sudden, it becomes diffuse; it's not in your stomach at all, it's everywhere in your aura. You lay down and you let go resisting this sensation. After about five minutes or so, it disappears. Then you can get up and walk away from it, and whether you eat or not is immaterial. At that point, you can eat!

The other trick to pull on it is to never allow yourself to get hungry. Anticipate—what time do you always get hungry? You get hungry at dinnertime—six o'clock, right? At 4:30, when you're not hungry, you have a piece of cheese and some crackers. At five o'clock, you have half of a banana. When dinner comes around, you are not even going to be hungry, since you just snacked when you weren't hungry, right? So, I call that "prophylactic eating." So, there is prophylactic eating, and letting go resisting it until you've unconditioned yourself to Pavlov's bell. You see, if you get a sensation and you label that hunger, then you feed it, now you just reinforced the Pavlovian conditioning. So, every time you eat when you're hungry, you reinforce the Pavlovian conditioning. Consequently, you can't get off of it; now you are at the effect of hunger. You're at the effect of the belief in hunger. The best that you can do is resist it and suffer and feel miserable, but you're not going to lose weight. You took off a few pounds, but I tell you, in a year it will be back, because you haven't changed the conditioning. It's simple: never eat when you are hungry; anticipate in advance when you're gonna be hungry; have something now when you're not hungry. If you're not hungry, half a hamburger will be quite satisfying if you're not hungry in the first place. Eat two hot dogs, one half of a lollipop, and you'll be satisfied.

See, the Buddha said, to sense, we become attached, and the Buddha emphasized the importance of detachment. To "detach" means to decondition yourself. It means to perceive of it, to understand what's happening from a different way, you know. So, I'm trying to explain it a different way. Never label it, never call it anything, never resist it, and it loses its power over you. And that way, you can go to the dentist and feel no pain. They can take off your—they can do an orthopedic amputation, and you experience no pain at all. But the instant you resist it or call it "pain," then it's very severe. Hmm. As they munch on the bone, you can shriek right through the ceiling. That comes from resisting it.

Pain Is One Thing; Suffering Is Another

So, when we get to meditative techniques, we'll talk more about the "now" of riding the crest of the moment. The minute you label a thing, anticipate it, or resist it, you're off the crest of the moment. If you stay in the exact moment of "now" means you cannot resist anything whatsoever, then you're in a very high space and you can transcend vertically in an instant into a great space. Then you're beyond suffering. To suffer is to resist the wave. Pain is one thing; suffering is another. They're not the same thing at all. You have to recondition your mind. Pain is one thing; suffering is something else. It's possible to experience incredible pain without any suffering. And it's possible to suffer a great deal without actually being in pain. So you dissociate the two things. Suffering is the resistance of that which is painful, but when you let go resisting pain, it loses its capacity to cause you to suffer. Anybody who's ever had narcotics knows that. If you ever had a gallbladder attack and they give you a shot of opium, it's incredible. The pain is still there, but it doesn't bother you in the slightest. You don't even care if it's there, because it's not you, you're not suffering from it, and it's a delightful and miraculous state. And you can see why opium was called many years ago—or morphine was called "God's own medicine"—because it took you out of the suffering, but the pain still was there. So, it's a dissociating. So, pain is one thing; suffering is another. And letting go resisting things is the way out of the pain of anything.

Q: *"What does Mother Teresa calibrate at?"*

Mother Teresa calibrates at 700. She has enormous heart. I experienced the truth of her when I was, uh . . . I went into an incredible state and after that, I couldn't practice for some time. But I then slowly went back after some period of time. What actually happened was, very severe cases came from all over the world. I eventually ended up with the biggest psychiatric practice in the United States, actually. Two thousand outpatients, a thousand new patients a year. I had 50 employees, 26 offices, laboratories, research laboratories, et cetera. And I had a huge hospital practice as well. And into the hospital came the worst possible cases given up by everybody—hopeless. And some incredible, just to witness them. They'd be wound up in wet sheets, brought in manacles from Maryland or someplace, and this writhing body would be put on the floor. And then they were instantly seen through the eyes, seeing the Self—seeing the Self of the entity within this psychotic mess. Instantly, there was like a healingness. The healingness was of the Spirit within. And at that point, the entity within couldn't have cared less about the state of the mind/body. It, like, realized its own truth, and in that instant, there was a healing. Which was what Mother Teresa did. She looked into the soul of the ugly dying of leprosy. Yes, precisely the same phenomena. So therefore, I understood her heart. So, when I wrote her, you know, she wrote me back, and there was like an awareness of the level out of which her heart was coming. It was like an awareness of heart there. She understood heart, you know. The lecture I'm giving today, she'd probably be bored with it, "Why do you talk about such things when they're not necessary?" Because if you can come through a heart that calibrates at 700, of course, who needs it? But that's a different lecture. We're not talking about the heart today. I don't want anybody loving anybody until the lecture on Heart.

Q: "I'm confused about if my body is involved with karma running itself, then how am I supposed to have spiritual experiences within this body if I identify with it?

Well, because you're not the body. So, the condition of the body, or whether you identify with the body is really irrelevant to your spiritual evolution. We would say that karmically, you've inherited the necessity, by having a physical body, to overcome those residuals from the body's evolution through the animal kingdom. Everybody here has to learn how to handle hunger, anger, fear, loss, defense, aggression, because everybody here has a physical body; and for it to survive, certain things then will tend to persist, yeah? So, there is a certain necessity then that befalls anyone who has a human body, just emanating from their bodyness itself, right? And to correct all those propensities is what we talked about this morning, because they translate into the positionalities of the ego, and as you let them go, the identification with the body disappears. When that does, whether it survives or not is really immaterial. Whether it dies or whether it gets blown up is immaterial. I remember, because I'd had that experience at age 12—in the navy, minesweepers are blowing up and falling and going down in the typhoons, et cetera, and there wasn't the slightest fear of anything at all. In fact, I was in a joyful state all the time. High as hell. And if you died, great. I mean, there was no identification with the body. So, the bodyness does not hold you back; it's only your identification with the bodyness—just as it isn't the ego that's holding you back; it's your identification with the ego. So you don't have to undo or destroy the ego; you just have to stop identifying with it as who you are.

CONCLUSION

We trust that you have been encouraged with the material given in this volume and that Dr. Hawkins's enlightening principles spur you upon your spiritual path.

The Truth is powerful and will change your life; with intention, dedication, willingness, and a devotion to God and the Truth, great strides can be made.

The following points are some of the inspiring Truths in this book that you can ponder for further understanding as you go through your day:

- In the Field of Consciousness, the only reality is light, and light is either present or not present, showing in varying degrees on the levels of consciousness.

- The Map of Consciousness® is like a prism that breaks up the light into different colors.

- The Levels of Consciousness are progressive levels of power within the field of consciousness. The higher you go, the greater the power.

- The ego is self-perpetuating, and it gets its energy out of the way it juices the lower positions.

- Spiritual work is making positive choices that will move you up toward the Light.

- If you are devoted to reaching some degree of enlightenment, you do not have time to check out the astral circus. Curiosity can lead one astray and waste valuable time.

- Certain information itself is transformational because it is so powerful.

- What the ego experiences is content and what Enlightenment is concerned with is context. God is the ultimate, infinite context; all of existence is content.

- Love is really the dawning of the light of the Presence of God within human consciousness in the nonlinear domain.

- Forgiveness is particularly important in spiritual work, being merciful toward ourselves, harmonious with others; being accepting of ourselves and others without condemning them.

- The whole point of this Scale of Consciousness, what we learn from it, is to support the intention on the part of everyone here to move forward in consciousness and to fulfill the human potential.

- That which you are, has a more profound effect on everything than that which you do.

- The most important thing that determines your level of consciousness is your spiritual intention.

As Dr. Hawkins often told us, the repetition of reading or hearing certain information can bring deeper meaning within one's consciousness. Read this book repeatedly, watch or listen to the lectures that are available and great insights will occur.

Straight and narrow is the path,
waste no time.
Gloria in Excelsis Deo!

ABOUT THE AUTHOR

David R. Hawkins, M.D., Ph.D. (1927–2012), was director of the Institute for Spiritual Research, Inc., and founder of the Path of Devotional Nonduality. He was renowned as a pioneering researcher in the field of consciousness as well as an author, lecturer, clinician, physician, and scientist. He served as an advisor to Catholic and Protestant churches, and Buddhist monasteries; appeared on major network television and radio programs; and le ctured widely at such places as Westminster Abbey, the Oxford Forum, the University of Notre Dame, and Harvard University. His life was devoted to the upliftment of mankind until his death in 2012.

For more information on Dr. Hawkins's work, visit **veritaspub.com**.

Hay House Titles of Related Interest

YOU CAN HEAL YOUR LIFE, the movie,
starring Louise Hay & Friends
(available as an online streaming video)
www.hayhouse.com/louise-movie

THE SHIFT, the movie,
starring Dr. Wayne W. Dyer
(available as an online streaming video)
www.hayhouse.com/the-shift-movie

***

THE AWAKENED WAY: Making the Shift to a Divinely Guided Life,
by Suzanne Giesemann

CONSCIOUSNESS IS ALL THERE IS: How Understanding and Experiencing Consciousness Will Transform Your Life, by Dr. Tony Nader

E-SQUARED: Nine Do-It-Yourself Energy Experiments That Prove Your Thoughts Create Your Reality, by Pam Grout

INTENTIONALITY: A Groundbreaking Guide to Breath, Consciousness, and Radical Self-Transformation, by Finnian Kelly

All of the above are available at your local bookstore,
or may be ordered by contacting Hay House (see next page).

***

We hope you enjoyed this Hay House book. If you'd like to receive our online catalog featuring additional information on Hay House books and products, or if you'd like to find out more about the Hay Foundation, please contact:

Hay House LLC, P.O. Box 5100, Carlsbad, CA 92018-5100
(760) 431-7695 or (800) 654-5126
www.hayhouse.com® • www.hayfoundation.org

———

Published in Australia by:
Hay House Australia Publishing Pty Ltd
18/36 Ralph St., Alexandria NSW 2015
Phone: +61 (02) 9669 4299
www.hayhouse.com.au

Published in the United Kingdom by:
Hay House UK Ltd
The Sixth Floor, Watson House,
54 Baker Street, London W1U 7BU
Phone: +44 (0) 203 927 7290
www.hayhouse.co.uk

Published in India by:
Hay House Publishers (India) Pvt Ltd
Muskaan Complex, Plot No. 3,
B-2, Vasant Kunj, New Delhi 110 070
Phone: +91 11 41761620
www.hayhouse.co.in

———

Let Your Soul Grow

Experience life-changing transformation—one video
at a time—with guidance from the world's leading experts.

www.healyourlifeplus.com